C0-ASI-569

JOSIE McCARTHY'S

Favorite TV Recipes

JOSIE McCARTHY'S
Favorite TV Recipes

by

Josephine McCarthy

Englewood Cliffs, N.J.

PRENTICE-HALL, INC.

To
Millie, Jodie, and Teresa
with all my love

PRENTICE-HALL, INC.
Englewood Cliffs, N.J.

LIBRARY OF CONGRESS CATALOG CARD NO.: 58-8544

PRINTED IN THE UNITED STATES OF AMERICA

51116

Contents

1. *Introduction*

I've loved to cook since I was a child. I made my first lemon meringue pie when I was seven years old. Since then I have made perhaps 147,000 more lemon meringue pies, none of which tasted half so good or gave me half so big a thrill as that first one.

But that was beginner's luck—or a child's illusion. If I have learned one thing in my many years with NBC—and earlier with Childs and Schraffts—it is that practice makes the cook.

Organization and patience are the two most important things in attacking a new dish. Naturally, with my television experience, I demonstrate my recipes in a step-by-step routine, always keeping a clear highway while working.

I get all the ingredients out first. The little cups, bowls, and jars are on paper towels. Then, for me, as it should be for the home cook, there is no scurrying to the cupboard, fumbling in the back of the refrigerator, or discovering that there is one important ingredient missing.

I also get out all the utensils. You often hear it said that men make better cooks than women. Maybe it is because most men devise ways of having their gadgets in plain view, usually hanging on handy hooks, while too many women have to dig into some drawer for the needed long fork, beater, or tongs.

So much for organization. Now for the patience and practice. It is my experience that it takes even a professional cook at least six tries to make a perfect dish. So I suggest that no housewife try any recipe for the first time when her husband's boss is coming to dinner.

The Million Dollar Cheese Cake recipe is almost foolproof, but I still recommend that before you make it for one of your show-off dishes you have a dress rehearsal as we do for every new dish we show on the program. Studio personnel make up my tasting committee. Your family can do the same for you.

Success in cooking requires self-confidence. I have encountered a surprising amount of reluctance among women to tackle any recipe that calls for yeast. This is silly. Yeast is simple to use, and opens up an entirely new field to the home cook. That many women have learned to overcome that reluctance is proved by the fact that the Chocolate Yeast Cake is the most popular dessert exhibited on our show. We are now getting more than 15,000 requests a year for it.

These recipes were chosen from thousands of the most popular presented to the public via TV during the past eight years. You will find them unusual, but in the main practical. Many are old-fashioned, slow to make, but, to my mind, worth the trouble. All of them will turn out delicious dishes that never go out of style.

The chocolate cake recipe was culled from the 20,000 that

we have offered on the air. I have chosen the recipes that draw the most requests year in and year out: the people's choice.

You will need to plan on time to prepare many of these recipes. Many are quick, but imaginative and different. For those who wish to deck the table lavishly with little time and practically no effort, I recommend the modern convenience foods. They have often helped me out in my rushed and busy schedule. The variety of convenience foods on the market today is a miracle of the era. They, with the modern kitchen appliances, have done away with the long hours of stirring, paring, and kneading and the big loads of dishes, pots, and pans. The convenience foods make it possible for inexperienced cooks, career women, and busy mothers to serve their families treats such as perfect fluffy cakes, luscious desserts, hot breads, vegetables, fruits and fish out of season, and whole dinners of foreign origin, to mention just a few. Yes, the convenience foods with their built-in maid services are one of the bright spots on a modern woman's horizon. Convenience or prepared food recipes are not included here, since they all carry explicit, foolproof package directions for serving. But there's room for imagination in serving these miracle foods. These have not been discussed here, however, because imagination is a personal thing, and evidence shows that none is lacking in the present-day use of prepared foods.

This book is a collection of ageless recipes, needing no unusual equipment. Only a few of them make use of the electric mixer, or blender, or other gadgets found in the average kitchen.

These recipes are for those who wish to re-create a gustatory memory or satisfy an urge for a dish seldom eaten. Each recipe is a cooking adventure. One of them included in a meal could point the repast up as something "special" and delightful. Each recipe was sampled and relished many times. You will treasure them as your own priceless collection.

HINTS

Here are some tried and true tips still in use today, as they were in our grandmother's day.

To **make fine dry bread crumbs,** place heels of bread, leftover rolls, etc., on baking pan in 250°F. slow oven for 1 hour. Cool. Place in plastic or heavy paper bag; pound and roll on the outside until crumbs are fine. Store in covered jar or container at room temperature.

To **clarify or sweeten fat** used in frying, reheat fat slowly with one sliced raw potato; when potato begins to color, remove from heat; cool until fat is still liquid but not too hot; strain through wire strainer or colander lined with 3 to 4 thicknesses of cheese-cloth.

To **remove fat from broth or soup,** lay one or two dry outside lettuce leaves on surface of broth for about 10 minutes; lift out leaves with fat clinging to them and discard. Repeat if needed.

To get a few drops of **juice from an onion,** cut a large peeled onion in half; spread surface with salt; scrape along cut surface with knife blade or teaspoon held over small square of foil, scraping onion juice onto the foil.

To **clarify tea,** add a few drops of boiling water to cloudy cold tea and watch it clear instantly.

To **bake an even pie shell** without fussing to keep the pastry from sliding down, for each pie shell choose two pie pans (any metal) of identical size. Invert both pans; fit the rolled-out pastry over one upside down pan; gently press all around to follow the pan's contour; trim excess pastry flush to the rim. Place second pie pan gently, but firmly, over the crust, sandwiching the crust in between the two pans. Bake upside down in hot oven, 425°F., 12 to 14 minutes; peek at crust by gently lifting off top pan; when crust is straw-colored, remove top pan. Continue baking until crust is baked a golden brown. Cool upside down; invert; fill. Pastry will have no fluted edge, but will be even with a minimum of fuss; each serving then will be less that much pastry.

Always continue stirring thick pie or cake fillings as they cool, to **prevent a tough skin forming** on top.

If you know you're going to be baking a cake that requires butter or margarine, take the amount of shortening you'll need out of the refrigerator and leave it at room temperature several hours before you'll need it; it will mix into your cake batter much more efficiently.

Before **freezing chopped meat** intended for hamburgers, shape the patties; stack with a square of foil or freezer paper between each patty. Then you won't have to wait for the whole block of meat to thaw in order to shape them when you want to cook a few or the whole batch.

When you need **gravy in a hurry** with no visible ingredients to make it, do this: allow 2 bouillon cubes dissolved in 1 cup of boiling water for each cup of gravy needed. Bring to a boil; add 1 grated raw medium potato and 1 teaspoon butter or margarine for each 2 cups bouillon; cover and cook until potato particles have cooked and dissolved into bouillon while thickening it into a gravy. Add a pinch of chili powder for use with beef; thyme for chicken; and rosemary for lamb or pork. Quick and wonderful!

To **measure butter or margarine** without using a cup, when butter or margarine is in 1/4 lb. prints, count each print as ½ cupful. If the pound of butter is in one block, one quarter of the block is ½ cupful. To measure 1 tablespoon, mark off each ¼ lb. into 8 pats; each pat is 1 tablespoon.

To grease cake, tart, and muffin pans with no paper lining needed, do this: mix together ½ cup unsalted shortening and 4 to 5 tablespoons flour until well blended; spread a visible film of this mixture evenly on insides of pan before putting in batter. Use a thicker coating for fruit muffins or batter you know will tend to stick to the pan. Invert cakes or muffins onto racks immediately on removing from oven. Keep some of this pan-grease mixture in a covered container near your baking things, not in the refrigerator.

To **prepare celery hearts** the day before a big party, cut scraped, trimmed, and thoroughly cleaned celery hearts into sixths or eighths; rinse in a bowl of cold water and lemon juice (1 quart of water and ¼ cup lemon juice); drain well; wrap celery in bunches of 8 or 10 in foil or freezer paper; refrigerate where there is no danger of freezing, making sure the celery lies straight. It will keep white and crisp this way until ready to serve.

When **freezing homemade ice cream,** spoon mixture into paper cup muffin pan liners; stand cups in freezer tray. Cover all with waxed paper. This makes individual serving portions.

For attractive, **savory baked potato skins,** rub outside of raw washed and dried potato with fat or oil before baking.

To keep from crying when **peeling a quantity of onions,** pour boiling water to cover onions in bowl or saucepan; let stand 3 to 4 minutes. Drain; cover with cold water; then peel. Absolutely no tears.

Always **thoroughly cool cooked chicken**, chicken broth, turkey, poultry stuffing, or milk and egg custards or fillings before refrigerating. Funny things happen when warm chicken broth, chicken dishes, or custards are put into the refrigerator; the chicken broth will turn sour overnight; the custards and fillings develop a bitter flavor. When in a hurry to cool foods, stand them in cold water, changing the water repeatedly.

To **whip cream,** use heavy cream containing a minimum of 30 per cent butterfat. Thoroughly chill the bowl and the beater intended for whipping the cream except in very cold weather. Turn cream into chilled bowl, and whip at once; do not overbeat; overbeating causes curdling. Return the whipped cream at once to the refrigerator. At serving time, spoon out the whipped cream without further stirring, discarding the small amount of milk that usually settles on the bottom when standing.

To **serve crisp cool salads,** have all ingredients cold. At serving time, turn them into a chilled salad bowl to keep the greens cold.

About salting: it's better to salt sparingly and have salt on the table for those who might like more. If your hand should slip and you oversalt a soup, there's an old hint that's still good today; that is, add a sliced raw potato to the boiling soup (if it can take a little more boiling), cook 5 to 6 minutes, and lift out and discard the potato.

A word **about pots and pans.** What kind of pots and pans are the best? This is often asked of me. The answer is to keep in mind your own particular requirements. Stainless steel is pretty, stays shiny, is easy to clean, and will not only last a lifetime, but can become an heirloom. Stainless steel, however, is not the best heat conductor. Since we depend on the heat entering the cooking food from the bottom, the best stainless steel utensils are the ones with aluminum, copper, or laminated-steel bottoms. These special bottoms will give a good even distribution of heat.

Copper pots and pans are excellent, but they need constant care to keep them bright.

Aluminum pots and pans are reliable, dependable, and excellent; they will cook evenly on any kind of stove or range because aluminum conducts the heat, and spreads the heat with no hot spots. Cast aluminum is durable and will not dent as will ordinary aluminum pots. Aluminum needs special care to keep it bright, but there are so many cleaners for it today that this is no longer much of a chore. Care must be taken not to use strong alkali materials on aluminum, however (for example, ammonia and washing or baking soda); they darken aluminum without causing any harmful effect in food cooked in the darkened pots. Some foods cooked in aluminum cause it to darken. Merely polishing the pan or cooking an acid food, or boiling cream of tartar or vinegar solution in the pot, will turn the dark color back to bright. Many aluminum pots and pans have lids with an anodized copper finish, and some cast aluminum utensils are covered with porcelain enamel in colors. Here a homemaker has to choose to fit her mode of living.

Cast iron is excellent for frying pans or Dutch ovens, since they hold, conduct, and spread the heat evenly. The iron pots and pans pose a problem. They rust when not in use. My mail brings questions on this repeatedly.

Here's **how to care for your iron frying pans** or skillets and Dutch ovens: after washing, dry them thoroughly, preferably over slow heat; cool. Rub them over completely with oil or fresh clean fat containing no salt. Then wipe off the excess fat or oil. They will take on a satiny gloss. Store them this way. Before using, wash off this fat coating as fat turns rancid on standing and even a little bit will give an off-flavor to food.

Iron skillets or frying pans used for cooking fatty foods or frying often don't get stuck up with food and don't need washing; just wipe them clean with paper and store; since they already have a slight fat coating, do not rub them with fat.

Before using new iron pots and pans, rub them with oil or unsalted fat and heat them quite hot; wash in soap or detergent and water; rinse; dry; oil, and wipe them; then use. Some cast iron casseroles, frying pans, and Dutch ovens are covered with enamelware, and the problem of their rusting does not exist. These are "extra" pieces to be added and are especially nice for both cooking and serving.

Heat-proof glass pots and ovenware are desirable because they don't lose their gloss, they don't impart any flavor to foods, and they let you see inside without having to peek under a cover. Glass is excellent for cooking acid fruits and berries. Cooking in glass is permissible where dietary laws of certain religious groups govern food preparation and cooking utensils. Glass is considered by them as "clean."

But glass utensils need care on the electric range; they should never be put directly on the heated grids. There is a special wire rack which is mandatory when cooking with glass on electric ranges; just slip it over the grid and place the pot on it. Care must be taken with glass so as not to subject it to sudden changes. For instance, one cannot pour boiling water out of a glass pot and immediately fill it with cold water, for it will crack. Cool that same pot and then add cold water, and all is well. The glass baking dishes and casseroles are most desirable because they can be used as serving dishes and can be put directly on the table. Glass casseroles come in a variety of shapes and colors with a variety of stands, some with candles for holding the food hot; these are excellent for buffet service.

Porcelain and earthenware are also in use today. Here a homemaker should choose the pieces that particularly fit her style of living.

2. *Soups*

Why don't we prepare home-made soup once in a while? What has happened to the glorious home-made soups of our mother's day? Prepared soups are a convenience, to be sure; they make soup possible at a moment's notice without any planning. By all means, let's give the ready-to-serve soups their due, but let's not lose the art of making soup ourselves, to our own taste, using our own inventive or imaginative touch. Why? There are three excellent reasons.

First—when we make soup at home, we make it in a large quantity. There are always at least two bowls for a serving. We can make the soup so nutritious that those two or more bowls can be the main course of the meal. It's a meal that contains good protein material, and, with a huge salad and a glorious dessert, meets any nutrition standards.

Second—home-made soup is economical. It's a perfect outlet for portions of leftover meat, fish, or vegetables. A tasty soup made at home can be the by-product of several meals, and thus does not add to the weekly food budget.

Third—home-made soups, lovingly made, can fit the individual family taste preference down to the last grain of pepper or other spice.

Besides these three important reasons for a home-maker to make a pot full of savory soup once in a while, it certainly can be a matter of pride to the cooking lady, and boost her morale and self-esteem so that, with little effort expended, she can personally contribute nutrition and pleasure to her family.

GREEK LAMB SOUP

- 4 tablespoons butter or margarine
- ¾ lb. lean shoulder lamb, diced in ½-inch squares
- 1 medium onion, chopped
- 1½ tablespoons flour
- 2 to 3 teaspoons curry powder
- 4 bouillon cubes
- 6 cups water
- ¾ cup raw regular rice
- 1 teaspoon salt
- ¼ teaspoon ground black pepper
- 1 teaspoon sugar
- 1 teaspoon mint flakes
- ½ teaspoon garlic salt
- 2 hard-cooked egg yolks

Melt butter in medium kettle or saucepan over moderate heat. Add lamb and onion; cook about 12 to 15 minutes, or until beginning to brown, stirring often. Stir in flour and curry powder; cook about 5 minutes, stirring frequently. Add bouillon cubes and water. Cover and simmer 1 hour. Add rice, salt, pepper, and sugar. Cover and simmer about 18 to 20 minutes, or until rice is tender. To serve, combine and blend mint flakes with garlic salt and egg yolks and press through a fine sieve onto top of soup. Makes 6 servings.

MANHATTAN CLAM CHOWDER

The reason the Manhattan Clam Chowder recipe is in the book stems from the fact that one day I made New

England Clam Chowder, and when I got requests for it, they said, "Please send me the Manhattan Clam Chowder too, the one with tomatoes in it." I make Clam Chowder "by ear"—but to put it down so that someone who never cooked could follow it, well, I had to do a little testing. I don't know how many cookbooks I've thumbed through to find a Manhattan Clam Chowder recipe—all I could find were just a couple. Basically, they were all the same—really a vegetable soup with chopped clams in it. But it's mighty good and I think you'll find this one a little different because it has just a soupçon of flavor from the cumin seed. Cumin, by the way, is a very popular spice. It is popular in Mexico and it is an ingredient—an important ingredient—in Mexican chili powder.

18 to 24 chowder clams in the shell, scrubbed clean
1 cup water
¼ lb. bacon or salt pork, diced
2 medium onions, chopped
3 celery stalks, diced
1 medium green pepper, diced
3 cups boiling water
2 cups canned tomatoes and liquid
2 medium potatoes, diced
1 cup water
1 teaspoon salt, or more to taste
¼ teaspoon ground black pepper
¼ teaspoon ground thyme leaves
1 teaspoon ground cumin seed
2 tablespoons chopped parsley

Place scrubbed clams in shells in kettle or saucepan with 1 cup water over moderate heat. Cover and steam until all the clams open. Cool, remove clams from shells, and retain broth in bottom of kettle. Discard shells and chop or grind clams fine; set aside. Meanwhile, fry bacon or salt pork until crisp. Add onions, celery, and green pepper and cook until soft. Add to clam broth in kettle. Add boiling water and tomatoes. Cover and simmer 45 minutes. Cook potatoes in 1 cup water with salt until barely tender; add and simmer 10 minutes. Add pepper, thyme, cumin seed, and ground clams. Simmer 5 minutes; add parsley, salt as needed, and serve with crackers. Makes approximately 6 large servings.

☙ BLACK MUSHROOM SOUP AU CHABLIS

When this soup made its bow on TV, my narrative went something like this: "There are soups that nourish and give a comfortable warm feeling . . . they definitely take the edge from the appetite. But here's a soup, clear and thin, that sharpens the appetite's edge and prepares the palate for good food to follow. We all know mushrooms are valued for their flavor. This soup condenses that good mushroom taste to the point where we can call it 'Essence of Mushrooms.' The aroma is most enticing. The lingering flavor it leaves on the palate sets it apart from ordinary run-of-the-mill soups. To my mind, the woman who doesn't serve Essence of Mushroom Soup to the family and guests is missing a great deal of fun . . . the fun of making it . . . the fun of joining in the joy of eating the results of her (not too strenuous) labor."

¼ cup butter or margarine
1 stalk celery, chopped
½ cup chopped onion
1 leek, chopped
1 carrot, grated
1 clove garlic, minced
1 lb. fresh mushrooms, chopped
1 tablespoon canned Italian-style tomato paste
2 tablespoons flour
2 tablespoons fat
6 chicken bouillon cubes
2 quarts boiling water
1 teaspoon salt
1 to 2 whole cloves
1 bay leaf
3 to 4 peppercorns
1 to 2 small fresh pork bones
¼ cup chablis
Croutons

Heat butter in large kettle or saucepan. Add vegetables and tomato paste. Cook over low heat until dark brown and dry, about ½ hour, stirring frequently. Stir in flour. Add fat, bouillon cubes, boiling water, seasonings, and pork bones. Cover and simmer 2 hours. Strain, cool, and chill. Lift solidified fat off the top and discard. Add chablis, bring to quick boil, and serve with croutons. Makes 6 servings.

COLD CRAB AND POTATO CREAM SOUP

- 4 tablespoons butter or margarine
- 4 to 5 leeks, chopped
- 1½ cups diced raw potatoes
- 2 cups hot water
- 1 teaspoon salt
- 2 cups milk
- ⅛ teaspoon ground white pepper
- 1 can (6½ oz.) crab meat, flaked
- 1 cup heavy cream
- Chopped chives

Melt butter or margarine in skillet over moderate heat. Add leeks and cook, stirring frequently until soft, about 15 to 20 minutes. Combine cooked leeks, potatoes, water, and salt in medium saucepan. Bring to a boil and simmer until potatoes are soft and break up easily. Whip smooth with rotary beater; add milk, pepper, and crab meat; bring to a boil. Remove from heat; add cream; cool and chill. Serve in bouillon cups with chopped chives sprinkled on top. Makes 6 servings.

SPINACH SOUP A L'EAU

- 1 minced shallot
- 4 tablespoons olive oil
- 1 lb. fresh spinach, coarsely chopped
- 1½ quarts boiling water
- 2 slices French bread, crumbled
- 1½ teaspoons salt
- ¼ teaspoon ground black pepper
- 2 egg yolks
- ½ cup heavy cream
- Lemon wedges

Cook shallot in oil in saucepan until straw-colored. Add spinach, water, French bread, salt and pepper. Cover and simmer 20 minutes. Combine egg yolks and cream in bottom of soup tureen. Pour hot soup over mixture, stirring briskly. Serve with lemon wedges. Makes 6 servings.

PHILADELPHIA PEPPER POT

6 beef bouillon cubes
2 quarts boiling water
½ lb. cooked fresh honeycomb tripe, diced
¼ teaspoon coarsely ground black pepper
2 bay leaves
½ cup chopped onion
½ cup diced celery
1 medium green pepper, diced
2 tablespoons butter or margarine
1 cup canned tomatoes
½ cup diced raw carrots
1 cup diced raw potatoes
½ cup uncooked elbow macaroni
1 teaspoon whole thyme leaves
1 teaspoon salt

Dissolve bouillon cubes in boiling water. Add tripe, pepper, and bay leaves. Cover and simmer 1 hour. Cook onions, celery, and green pepper in butter about 10 minutes or until soft and add to tripe. Add tomatoes and simmer ½ hour longer. Add carrots, potatoes, macaroni, thyme, and salt. Simmer ½ hour longer or until vegetables and macaroni are tender. Makes 6 servings.

CALICO SOUP WITH HAM DUMPLINGS

2 tablespoons chopped ham fat
1 medium onion, chopped
1½ cups washed green split peas
1 small ham shank
¼ cup chopped celery leaves
2 quarts cold water
2 teaspoons salt
¼ teaspoon ground black pepper
Ham dumplings

Cook ham fat in kettle until crisp. Add onion; brown lightly. Add split peas, ham shank, celery leaves, cold water, salt, and pepper. Cover and simmer until peas are soft enough to mash (about 2½ hours). Remove shank, cut off meat, and mince fine. Reserve ¾ cup for dumplings, and return remaining ham to soup. Add ham dumplings (see below) and simmer covered 12 to 15 minutes. Serve one dumpling in each dish of soup. Makes 6 servings.

Ham Dumplings

- 1 cup sifted all-purpose flour
- 2 teaspoons baking powder
- ¼ teaspoon salt
- ¾ cup chopped cooked ham
- ½ cup milk

Sift flour, baking powder, and salt together into mixing bowl. Add ham and milk. Stir to make soft dough. Drop by tablespoonfuls into boiling soup. Cover and simmer 12 to 15 minutes. Makes 6 large dumplings.

CHICKEN MULLIGATAWNY SOUP

- 1 (3 to 4 lbs.) ready-to-cook stewing chicken
- 2 quarts boiling water
- 3 whole cloves
- 2 teaspoons salt
- ¼ cup chopped onion
- ½ cup chopped green pepper
- 2 tablespoons butter or margarine
- 1 teaspoon curry powder
- ½ cup diced carrots
- 1 sour apple, peeled and chopped
- 2 tablespoons flour
- ½ cup canned tomatoes
- Hot cooked rice

Place chicken in large saucepan or kettle. Add water, cloves, and salt. Cover and simmer about 2½ to 3 hours until chicken is tender. Lift chicken from broth; reserve breast meat for use in salad or sandwiches. Cool broth. Remove bones and skin from remaining chicken; chop meat and set aside. Cook onions and green pepper in butter about 10 minutes or until soft; add curry powder. Skim fat from surface of broth. Return to heat; bring to a boil. Add cooked onions and green pepper, carrots, apple, and chopped chicken meat. Combine flour and tomatoes, stirring until smooth; stir into soup. Cover and simmer about ½ hour or until vegetables are tender. Serve with hot cooked rice in each serving. Makes 6 servings.

NOTE: To skim fat off broth, place 2 lettuce leaves on top for several minutes. Remove lettuce, to which fat has adhered.

GAZPACHO
(Cold Spanish Soup)

4 slices white bread
1 clove garlic, minced
1 onion, sliced thin
1 cucumber, shredded
2 green peppers, finely chopped
Salt
Freshly ground black pepper
Powdered dry mustard
1 tablespoon whole caraway seed
⅓ to ½ cup olive oil
2 tablespoons vinegar
Juice of ½ lemon
6 cups water
Ice cubes

Remove and discard crusts from bread; cut bread into cubes; place in a soup tureen. Sprinkle garlic, onion, cucumber, and peppers over bread in tureen. Season with salt, freshly ground pepper, and dry mustard. Add caraway seed. Dribble olive oil on top; mix thoroughly. Mix together vinegar, lemon juice, and water; pour over bread mixture. Chill thoroughly, 3 to 4 hours. To serve, float 6 or 8 ice cubes in mixture; ladle at the table from tureen into soup cups. Makes 6 to 8 servings.

YANKEE BEAN SOUP

1 lb. navy or pea beans
2½ quarts water
1 small ham or pork bone
1 large onion, sliced
½ cup chopped celery leaves
½ teaspoon dry mustard
3 tablespoons butter or margarine
1 small onion, finely chopped
2 medium carrots, finely diced
¾ cup canned tomatoes and liquid
2 to 3 teaspoons salt
Ground black pepper

Pick over beans; wash thoroughly. Place with water in large kettle over high heat; bring to a boil; reduce heat. Cover and cook 10 minutes. Remove from heat; let stand covered 1 hour. Add ham bone, onion, celery leaves, and mustard. Cover and simmer 1½ to 2 hours or until beans are soft but unbroken. Heat butter in skillet or frying pan over moderate heat until frothy; add onion and carrots; cook 6 to 7 minutes or until beginning to brown, stirring constantly. Add with tomatoes, salt, and pepper to beans. Cover and simmer 20 to 25 minutes or until beans are partly broken and have slightly thickened the soup. Remove ham bone before serving. Makes 6 to 8 servings.

BEET BORSCHT

4 medium-size beets and leafy tops
3 cups cold water
1 onion, grated
4 cups boiling water
1 tablespoon salt
3 tablespoons brown sugar
2 to 3 teaspoons sour salt
Hot boiled potatoes
Commercial sour cream

Cut leaves off beets; leave 2-inch stems. Scrub beets thoroughly; cover with cold water; boil covered 15 to 20 minutes. Wash beet leaves, discarding stems. Chop leaves fine;

set aside. Drain beets; reserve liquid; slip skins off beets; grate fine. Combine beet liquid, onion, boiling water, salt, chopped beet leaves, and grated beets in saucepan; cover and simmer over moderate heat 5 minutes. Add brown sugar and sour salt. Serve hot or cold with a hot boiled potato and 2 tablespoons thick sour cream in each serving. Makes 4 to 6 servings.

NOTE: If sour salt is not available, season to taste with salt and lemon juice.

◆§ SWEET CHERRY SOUP

- 1 lb. (2 cups) fresh sweet cherries
- 1 quart water
- ½ cup sugar
- ⅛ teaspoon salt
- 3 tablespoons quick-cooking tapioca
- 1 cup water
- 2-inch strip lemon peel
- 2 tablespoons fresh lemon juice
- ½ cup white wine
- Whipped cream, if desired

Stem, wash, and pit all but 18 cherries, reserving these cherries for garnish. Crack about 20 pits; set them aside. Place pitted cherries and water together in saucepan over moderate heat; cover and simmer 15 to 20 minutes or until cherries are tender enough to mash. Puree the cherries with their liquid by blending mixture in electric blender or rubbing through a sieve. Place the pureed cherries, sugar, salt, and tapioca together in saucepan over moderate heat; cover and simmer 30 to 35 minutes or until tapioca has softened and dissolved, thickening soup slightly. Meanwhile place together into small saucepan the cracked cherry pits and one cup water over moderate heat; cover and simmer 10 to 15 minutes; strain, discarding pits; add liquid to soup. Add lemon peel and juice, whole cherries, and more sugar if desired; remove from heat. Cool, covered, 5 to 10 minutes or until warm but not hot; remove lemon peel; add wine. Serve warm in cups as first course, or cold with spoonful of whipped cream in each cup as dessert. Makes 4 to 6 servings.

❧ SOUR CHERRY SOUP

1 lb. (2 cups) fresh sour red cherries
1 quart water
1-inch piece whole cinnamon
2-inch strip lemon peel
½ cup sugar
1 cup red Bordeaux wine
1 tablespoon cornstarch
¼ cup cold water
1 tablespoon sugar
⅛ teaspoon salt
½ cup whipped cream
¼ teaspoon vanilla, if desired
Lady fingers, if desired

Stem, wash, and pit all but 18 cherries, which should be reserved for garnish. Crack about 20 pits; set them aside. Place pitted cherries, water, cinnamon, lemon peel, and sugar together in saucepan over moderate heat. Cover and simmer 8 to 10 minutes. Remove cinnamon and lemon. Puree the cherries with liquid by blending 1 minute in electric blender or by rubbing through a sieve. Meanwhile, place cracked reserved cherry pits together with wine in small saucepan; cover and simmer 8 to 9 minutes over very low heat; strain, discarding pits. Combine cherry puree, strained wine, and whole unpitted cherries in saucepan; bring to a boil. Mix together cornstarch, water, sugar, and salt; slowly add to boiling mixture, stirring constantly; cook 2 to 3 minutes. Serve hot or warm in soup cups with spoonful of whipped cream in each cup for first course. For dessert, cool; add ¼ teaspoon vanilla; serve in cups with whipped cream on top and lady fingers on the side. Makes 4 to 6 servings.

3. *Vegetables*

How fortunate we are that we live in a land that gives us such a bountiful supply of vegetables and so great a variety. A well balanced meal should include at least one vegetable, beside potato, and a green leafy salad, as vegetables carry an abundance of vitamins and minerals needed in our everyday living.

Aside from the nutritive value, each vegetable gives us its own characteristic flavor, often a very delicate flavor, when prepared properly.

◆§ OVEN ROASTED CORN AND BACON

6 ears of tender corn
Salt
Chili powder
6 slices bacon

Remove husks and silk from fresh corn, or use frozen or canned corn on the cob. Rub each ear lightly with salt and chili powder. Spiral a strip of bacon around each corn ear and pin ends of bacon with a toothpick. Place on rack in roasting pan. Bake in a moderate oven (375°F.) 15 to 20 minutes or until bacon is cooked. Baste corn occasionally with bacon juices as they ooze out during cooking. Serve piping hot. Makes 6 servings.

☙ SQUASH PATTIES

Plain and fancy—that's what I say about this dish! Squash is plain enough but the treatment is rather fancy. The recipe calls for Italian green squash—zucchini—but you can make it with any tender squash—patty pan, any young tender-skinned variety, or the tender yellow crookneck squash. Squash is a gentle vegetable—gentle in flavor and texture, that is—and here the flavor is stepped up by the addition of Parmesan cheese and parsley and onion. Adding the eggs turns them into fritters. The studio gang turned these fritters into sandwiches and had themselves a delightful snack. After you've made them a few times you can experiment adding bits of ham, salami, or leftovers.

2 medium zucchini squash
1 cup soft bread crumbs
¼ cup grated Parmesan cheese
¼ cup grated onion
2 tablespoons chopped parsley
1 teaspoon salt
¼ teaspoon ground black pepper
2 eggs, beaten
Oil for pan-frying

Scrub zucchini. If gritty, peel lightly. Shred on vegetable shredder. There should be about 2 cupfuls. Combine shredded zucchini, bread crumbs, cheese, onion, parsley, salt, pepper, and eggs. Beat well. Drop by tablespoons into heated shallow oil in large skillet. Have oil about ¼ inch in depth. Cook over moderate heat until lightly browned; turn and brown on other side. Serve with meat or fish. Makes 8 small patties.

MEATLESS STUFFED ZUCCHINI

2 lbs. fresh zucchini (Italian green squash)
2 cups soft bread crumbs
¾ cup shredded American Cheddar cheese
1 egg, slightly beaten
¼ cup grated onion
¼ cup minced parsley
½ teaspoon salt
½ teaspoon ground black pepper
1 cup canned meatless spaghetti sauce, or canned tomatoes, or any gravy

Scrub zucchini, peel lightly if gritty, and trim off stem end. Cut zucchini into 3-inch lengths. Run an apple corer through the center of the zucchini lengthwise and pull out the cylinder thus loosened. Chop these zucchini cylinders very fine and add to bread crumbs. Add cheese, egg, onion, parsley, salt, and pepper. Mix well and pack into hollowed zucchini. Shape any remaining stuffing into small balls. Place zucchini and stuffing-balls in greased shallow baking dish. Sprinkle spaghetti sauce over all. Cover and bake in a hot oven (400°F.) 1 hour. Uncover and bake ½ hour longer. Makes 4 servings.

ZUCCHINI AND MUSHROOM PANCAKE

2 medium zucchini squash
⅓ cup salad oil
4 eggs, beaten
½ cup canned sliced mushrooms, drained
4 tablespoons grated Parmesan cheese
¾ teaspoon salt
⅛ teaspoon ground black pepper

Scrub zucchini; trim and cut across into ¼-inch slices. Heat oil in large skillet or frying pan over moderate heat; add zucchini and cook about 5 minutes, turning slices carefully until lightly browned. Mix together eggs, mushrooms, cheese, salt, and pepper; pour over zucchini; lower heat and cook about 4 to 5 minutes, or until set but still moist, without stirring. Place skillet 4 to 5 inches from broiler heat; broil about 3 to 4 minutes or until slightly puffed and browned. Cut into wedges at once and serve. Makes 4 servings.

NOTE: This is a fine luncheon or supper dish. It can be used as a hot sandwich filling. It can be cut into bite-sized pieces and served on crackers or toast rounds as a hot cocktail snack.

◆§ SCALLOPED TOMATOES

It's about time scalloped tomatoes made a come-back. Could it be that the old version of boarding house stewed tomatoes and bread put them in bad repute? I've heard women say they wished the horticulturists would grow about twenty more new vegetables, but since that is not likely to happen, how about trying to do something different with this old stand-by? To me this is a beautiful recipe. Beautiful because it's not just thrown together. First, the bread is toasted slightly with onions that were cooked a bit to develop a deeper flavor. Then the mixture of the tomatoes and bread cooks until the bread has been entirely absorbed. Not a speck of bread shows in the finished dish. The tomatoes are glossy and slightly thickened. They make a beautiful accompaniment to fish or veal, pork, lamb, beef, or poultry. You'll be my friend for life if you give scalloped tomatoes another chance, using this recipe.

- 2 slices rye bread (with caraway seed)
- ½ cup chopped onion
- 3 tablespoons oil
- 2 cups canned tomatoes
- 1 teaspoon sugar
- Salt and ground black pepper to taste

Cut bread into ½-inch cubes and set aside. Cook onion in oil until soft, but not colored. Add bread and cook until lightly browned, stirring constantly. Place onion-bread mixture and tomatoes in small saucepan. Add sugar, salt, and pepper; cover and simmer 1 hour, stirring often. Makes 4 servings.

BROILED EGGPLANT STEAK

One of the most misunderstood vegetables today is eggplant. But, as with people, when you take the time to understand them, you'll like them. I'll guarantee that if you'll take the time to understand how to handle an eggplant and try it plain broiled like this, you'll say "Where have I been? I didn't know about eggplant being so good before. This is divine!"

1 medium eggplant (about 1½ lbs.)
Olive oil for brushing eggplant
Salt or garlic salt
Ground black pepper

Slice unpeeled eggplant crosswise into 1-inch slices. Place on broiler rack. Brush with olive oil. Sprinkle with salt and pepper. Broil 3 to 4 inches from heat about 5 to 6 minutes, or until slices begin to brown. Turn with pancake turner. Brush with oil and sprinkle with salt and pepper. Broil second side 5 to 6 minutes or until slices have softened and browned. Makes 4 servings.

WATERLESS COOKED BEETS WITH ONIONS

6 fresh medium beets, pared
3 tablespoons butter or margarine
2 medium onions, sliced
1 teaspoon sugar
2 teaspoons salt
⅛ teaspoon ground black pepper
Lettuce leaves
2 tablespoons cider vinegar or fresh lemon juice

Shred raw beets. Place butter in small saucepan. Add beets. Spread sliced onions over beets. Sprinkle with sugar, salt, and pepper. Cover completely with overlapping wet lettuce leaves. Cover and simmer 20 to 25 minutes, or until tender. Discard lettuce. Sprinkle with vinegar or lemon juice before serving. Makes 6 servings.

⇜ BRUSSELS SPROUTS WITH GRAPES

Good old Brussels sprouts! Eyebrows usually get raised when chestnuts are served with them, or mushrooms—but Brussels sprouts with Grapes! Who ever heard of such a thing! You'll find that folks who wouldn't eat them with chestnuts will try them with grapes and like them so well they'll eat the last speck—bit, that is. This recipe got into the book because it was very popular. We also thought you'd like a little "chi-chi" idea for serving this not too popular vegetable.

- 1½ lbs. fresh Brussels sprouts, or 2 packages frozen
- 1 cup malaga or tokay grapes
- 4 to 5 tablespoons melted butter or margarine

Trim, wash, and cook Brussels sprouts in boiling salted water until tender but not broken. Meanwhile cut grapes in half and remove seeds. Drain sprouts and add grapes. Cover and steam 5 minutes. Add melted butter or margarine. Serve with meat, fish, or poultry. Makes 6 servings.

⇜ SPANISH CAULIFLOWER

Did you ever go into an Italian restaurant where they wheeled out a cart laden down with antipasto and you took your pick from anchovies, sardines, salami, hard-cooked eggs, celery, tuna and other pickled fish, and numerous dishes of cold cooked vegetables of all kinds in a nice snappy sauce? This Spanish Cauliflower is one of those dishes. It's just as good cold as it is hot. If you want to put it on a buffet table or take it to a picnic you can serve it with cold cuts or cold spiced fish.

- 1 medium head cauliflower, washed and drained
- 2 cups water
- 1½ teaspoons salt
- 1 onion, chopped
- 1 clove garlic, minced
- ¼ cup olive oil
- 2 tablespoons wine vinegar
- 2 tablespoons water
- 1 teaspoon sugar
- ¼ teaspoon ground black pepper

Break cauliflower into flowerets, discarding center core and leaves. Cover and boil in water and salt about 15 minutes. Drain. Cook onion and garlic in oil in saucepan until golden. Add vinegar, water, sugar, and pepper. Cook 3 to 4 minutes. Add cauliflower; stir lightly; cover and simmer about 10 minutes, or until cauliflower is tender. Serve hot as a vegetable with fish or meats. Serve cold as an appetizer with anchovies. Makes 4 to 6 servings.

❧ TOP-OF-THE-STOVE STUFFED GREEN PEPPERS

In the good old summertime when Bell peppers are selling for pennies, that's the time to get your splurge of peppers and then not feel deprived when they go to 15 to 25 cents apiece in the middle of winter. Isn't it marvelous that you can cook stuffed peppers without having to light the oven? These are done all on top of the stove. And unlike the regular stuffed peppers—the ones done in the oven—you can eat the whole pepper. So many times with the oven-baked, you can't eat the pepper itself—only the stuffing.

The firm, thick pepper walls don't seem to cook tender in the dry heat as they do in the atmosphere of steam. With this recipe, you can eat the whole thing.

6 medium green peppers
1 cup chopped onion
1 cup soft bread crumbs
¼ cup grated Parmesan cheese
½ teaspoon salt
⅛ teaspoon ground black pepper
1 egg, beaten
3 tablespoons olive oil
½ cup tomato juice or water
1 tablespoon fresh lemon juice

Cut peppers in half lengthwise, remove seeds, rinse, and drain. Mix together onion, bread crumbs, cheese, salt, pepper, and egg; spoon into pepper halves. Place oil in large skillet or frying pan over low heat. Arrange filled peppers in skillet, rounded sides down. Add tomato juice or water, and lemon juice; cover and simmer over very low heat about 45 to 50 minutes or until tender. Lift off cover, raise heat, and let cook about 10 to 12 minutes or until liquid cooks down to a rich sauce. Serve hot as a vegetable, or cold for buffets. Makes 6 servings.

☙ TOP-OF-THE-STOVE CANDIED SWEET POTATOES

When we eat baked in the oven candied sweet potatoes, most of what we taste is the sugar. This recipe has a definite sweet potato or yam flavor. The reason is that the potato is not boiled in water which robs it of flavor. All the flavor remains right in the potato. Most cooks feel that sweet potatoes have to be boiled first. Well, experiments show that you can use raw sweet potatoes, grated or sliced, in a good many favorites like this and in some desserts. This recipe is a great help on a day like Thanksgiving, when the oven can't hold another thing. A few women have written that for this reason alone these candied sweets deserve honorable mention. They were quite surprised over the good flavor of the potatoes. There's really no precaution to getting this dish right except to work quickly and get the peeled potatoes right into the hot water before they have time to darken. Here again, you can add your own touch after you've made them one or twice and have gained confidence. You can add pecans or spices or chopped orange, and even use maple syrup instead of honey.

4 medium sweet potatoes or yams
Boiling water
⅛ teaspoon salt
⅓ cup honey

Pare raw sweet potatoes or yams and slice ½ to 1 inch thick. Slice small potatoes lengthwise and large ones crosswise. Place potatoes in a large skillet or frying pan. Add enough boiling water to cover. Add salt and honey. Cover and simmer 25 minutes. Remove cover; turn potatoes and boil until the liquid has evaporated down to a syrup. Gently turn potatoes several times until they are glazed. Serve piping hot. Makes 4 servings.

SPINACH WITH GARLIC BREAD CRUMBS

1½ lbs. fresh spinach, washed
¾ teaspoon salt
4 tablespoons bacon fat, or butter or margarine
1 cup soft bread crumbs
1 clove garlic, crushed

Lift spinach from final washing water directly into medium saucepan; sprinkle salt on top; cover and steam over high heat 5 to 6 minutes, turning it as soon as it steams. Meanwhile, melt bacon fat in small skillet or frying pan over moderate heat; add bread crumbs and garlic. Cook 2 to 3 minutes, stirring constantly until golden brown. Drain spinach thoroughly; sprinkle browned garlic crumbs on top. Makes 6 servings.

❧ BAKED BROCCOLI AND SWISS CHEESE CUSTARD

3 cups diced cooked fresh broccoli
2 cups milk
3 eggs, slightly beaten
¾ cup shredded Swiss cheese
½ teaspoon celery salt
⅛ teaspoon ground black pepper
Paprika

Place broccoli in greased shallow baking dish. Stir milk into eggs. Add cheese, celery salt, and pepper. Pour over broccoli. Sprinkle with paprika. Bake in a moderate oven (350°F.) about 35 minutes, or until lightly browned and custard around broccoli is no longer liquid upon testing with tip of a knife. Makes 6 servings.

NOTE: Excellent with fish.

❧ CARROTS WITH BACON

4 carrots, washed and scraped
Boiling water, salted
4 slices bacon

Cook carrots, whole, in salted boiling water until tender but firm. Drain. Wrap 1 strip of bacon around each cooked whole carrot. Pin ends of bacon to carrots with toothpicks. Place on broiler rack. Broil, turning frequently until bacon is crisped. Serve hot. Makes 4 servings.

❧ MASHED POTATOES WITH CARROTS

3 cups mashed white potatoes
1 cup grated raw carrots
Salt and ground black pepper, to taste
Butter or margarine

Whip mashed potatoes until fluffy; combine with finely grated raw carrots, salt, and pepper; beat well. Place in greased baking dish; dot with butter or margarine. Bake in a hot oven (400°F.) about 15 minutes, or until lightly browned on top. Makes 4 servings.

PAN-FRIED SWISS STYLE POTATOES

- 4 tablespoons butter or margarine
- 3 large potatoes, pared, cut into match-like strips
- 1 teaspoon salt
- ⅛ teaspoon ground black pepper

Melt butter in large skillet over moderate heat. When frothy, add potatoes; spread evenly; add salt and pepper. Cover; lower heat and cook until tender. Uncover and cook until brown crust is formed on bottom. Loosen from pan with pancake turner. Invert, with brown crust uppermost, onto a dish slightly larger than the skillet and serve. Makes 4 to 6 servings.

NOTE: To brown on both sides, add another 2 tablespoons butter or margarine to skillet; add potatoes, brown side up, and cook uncovered until crusty and brown underneath.

SKILLET ASPARAGUS

- 1½ lbs. fresh asparagus
- 2 tablespoons salad oil
- ¾ teaspoon salt
- 2 tablespoons water
- 1 teaspoon cornstarch
- 1 tablespoon soy sauce
- ½ cup bouillon (use bouillon cube)

Cut off tough asparagus ends; remove scales from stalks; wash and drain. Slice asparagus very thin diagonally across the stalks and tips into 1- to 1½-inch long slices. Heat oil in large skillet or frying pan over moderate heat until hot but not smoking; add asparagus, salt, and water. Lower heat. Cover and cook 5 to 6 minutes over low heat, adding few drops water as needed until asparagus are done but still crisp. Mix together cornstarch, soy sauce, and bouillon; add to asparagus, stirring constantly. Cook uncovered 2 to 3 minutes, or until juices are slightly thickened and clear, stirring constantly. Makes 4 servings.

❧ SAUERKRAUT WITH RAISINS

- ¼ cup bacon fat or salad oil
- ½ cup chopped onion
- 1 can (1 lb. 11 oz.) sauerkraut
- 1 teaspoon whole celery seed
- 1 clove garlic, crushed
- ½ cup boiling water
- ½ cup boiling water for raisins
- ¾ cup raisins
- ½ cup grated raw potato
- 3 to 4 peppercorns

Place bacon fat and onions into saucepan; cook over moderate heat until onions are lightly browned, stirring frequently. Add sauerkraut, celery seed, garlic, and boiling water; cover and simmer 45 minutes, stirring occasionally. Pour boiling water over raisins in bowl; let stand 5 minutes; drain. Add raisins, raw potato, and peppercorns to sauerkraut, stirring well; cover and simmer 15 minutes. Serve hot. Makes 6 servings.

❧ BRAISED CHINESE CABBAGE

- 1 medium head Chinese cabbage
- 2 tablespoons butter or margarine
- ½ teaspoon salt
- 1 tablespoon flour
- 2 tablespoons soft butter or margarine
- Ground black pepper

Slice root end off cabbage; wash and drain. Slice across whole head of cabbage to make 1/4-inch thick strips. Heat butter in large skillet or frying pan over moderate heat until frothy. Add cabbage and salt. Cook, uncovered, 4 to 5 minutes or until steaming throughout, stirring often. Mix together flour and butter until blended. Add by half-teaspoonfuls to juices around cabbage in pan, stirring until slightly thickened gravy forms throughout. Add pepper to taste; serve at once. Makes 4 servings.

☙ VEGETABLE MIXED GRILL

1 medium eggplant
2 medium green or yellow squash, scrubbed
4 tomatoes
½ lb. large mushroom caps
Olive oil
Salt
Ground black pepper
Fine bread crumbs

Wash and slice unpeeled eggplant across into 1½-inch slices, discarding tip and stem ends. Cut unpeeled squash into halves lengthwise; scoop out seeds. Cut tomatoes across into halves. Wash and remove stems from mushroom caps; do not peel. Brush vegetables liberally on all sides with oil. Sprinkle with salt and pepper. Sprinkle cut surface of tomatoes with bread crumbs. Arrange eggplant and squash on rack in pre-heated broiler, 4 inches from heat. Broil 5 minutes, or until vegetables begin to brown. Turn over; place tomatoes, crumbed-side up, on rack. Broil 5 to 6 minutes, or until vegetables are golden brown and tender. Add mushrooms, rounded side down. Broil 2 to 3 minutes, or until juice flows and fills mushroom caps. Serve immediately as accompaniment to meat, fish, or poultry. Makes 4 servings.

HOME FRIED POTATOES

⅓ cup oil or any cooking fat
1 quart sliced cold boiled potatoes
¾ to 1 teaspoon salt
¼ teaspoon ground black pepper

Heat oil or fat in frying pan or skillet over low heat until hot but not smoking. Add sliced potatoes; spread to cover entire pan. Sprinkle with salt and pepper. Cook without turning 6 to 7 minutes or until bottoms of potatoes have turned a rich golden color. Loosen potatoes and turn over with pancake turner. Cook 5 to 7 minutes longer until browned on under side. Serve hot. Makes 4 servings.

CREAMED SLICED ONIONS AMANDINE

1 tablespoon butter or margarine
1 quart sliced onions
1 teaspoon salt
3 tablespoons butter or margarine
3 tablespoons flour
1 teaspoon salt
1½ cups milk
¾ cup soft bread crumbs
2 tablespoons melted butter or margarine
¼ cup slivered or chopped blanched almonds

Heat butter in saucepan over moderate heat until frothy; add onions and salt. Cover and simmer 12 to 15 minutes or until barely soft. Meanwhile heat remaining butter in saucepan over low heat until frothy. Stir in flour and salt. Gradually add milk, stirring until thickened and smooth; add to cooked onions, mixing thoroughly. Turn into greased shallow casserole. Mix together bread crumbs, butter, and almonds; sprinkle over onions. Bake in a moderate oven (375°F.) 25 to 30 minutes or until browned on top. Makes 4 to 6 servings.

STEAMED ZUCCHINI AND SALAMI

- 1½ to 2 lbs. fresh zucchini
- 3 tablespoons butter, margarine, or oil
- 4 slices Italian garlic salami, chopped
- ¼ teaspoon salt
- 6 to 8 green outside lettuce leaves
- 2 to 3 tablespoons grated Romano or Parmesan cheese

Wash, trim and scrub zucchini with a brush or pare lightly to remove any imbedded soil or grit. Slice across into ¼-inch thick rounds. Place butter in small saucepan; add zucchini, salami, and salt. Dip lettuce leaves into cold water; place on top to completely cover the food and to enclose steam as it cooks. Cover tightly and simmer over very low heat 18 to 20 minutes, or until tender. Lift off and discard lettuce leaves. Serve zucchini with cheese on top. Makes 4 servings.

SAVORY SWISS CHARD

- 1 lb. young fresh Swiss chard
- ½ teaspoon salt
- ½ teaspoon garlic salt
- 3 tablespoons olive oil
- 2 tablespoons fresh lemon juice
- ¼ teaspoon ground black pepper
- 2 tablespoons grated Parmesan or Romano cheese

Wash chard thoroughly. Cut stalks across into ½-inch thick pieces. Place in saucepan; arrange wet leaves on top; sprinkle with salt and garlic salt. Cover and cook 10 to 15 minutes or until crispy tender, over low heat, adding a few drops of water if needed. Remove from heat; cut criss-cross with 2 knives. Mix together oil, lemon juice, pepper, and cheese; add to chard, tossing until blended. Reheat 1 or 2 minutes before serving. Makes 4 servings.

BUTTERED ONIONS WITH WALNUTS

4 tablespoons butter or margarine
½ cup walnut halves
3 cups drained, seasoned, hot cooked or canned small onions

Heat butter in skillet or frying pan over low heat; add walnuts; cook 2 to 4 minutes or until lightly toasted, stirring constantly. Remove from heat. Turn onions into heated serving dish; place cooked walnuts on top. Lightly stir walnuts throughout onions. Makes 6 servings.

BRAISED ENDIVE

4 small heads Belgian endive
2 tablespoons oil or drippings
1 small clove garlic, minced
¾ cup bouillon
1 teaspoon cornstarch
Salt, to taste

Wash and trim endive. Slice off root-ends. Cut whole endives lengthwise into fourths. Heat oil in small saucepan over very low heat; add endive and garlic. Simmer 10 minutes, tightly covered. Mix together bouillon and cornstarch; pour over endive. Cover and simmer 20 minutes over low heat. Add salt to taste. Serve hot. Makes 4 servings.

GRATED POTATO AND CARROT KUGEL

4 raw medium potatoes, pared and grated (about 2 cupfuls)
¼ cup grated onion
¾ cup grated raw carrot
½ to ¾ teaspoon salt
¼ teaspoon ground black pepper
½ cup sifted flour
3 tablespoons melted shortening or salad oil
2 eggs, beaten

Mix together potatoes, onion, carrot, salt, and pepper with flour and melted shortening. Stir until well-blended and smooth. Add well-beaten eggs. Mix lightly but thoroughly; turn into greased shallow casserole. Bake in a moderate oven (375°F.) 45 minutes, or until toothpick inserted in center comes out clean. Serve hot, cut into squares; serve in place of potatoes. Makes 6 servings.

BUTTERED OKRA

1 lb. fresh or frozen okra
2 cups boiling water
½ teaspoon salt
¼ teaspoon onion salt
2 tablespoons melted butter or margarine

Wash, drain, and cut stem ends off fresh okra pods (packaged frozen okra is fully trimmed). Place into water. Add salt. Cover and simmer 20 to 25 minutes, or until tender. Drain; add onion salt and butter. Toss lightly and serve as a vegetable with meat, fish, or poultry. Makes 4 servings.

CREAMED SALSIFY (OYSTER PLANT)

1 bunch (1½ to 1¾ lbs.) salsify
2 cups cold water
¼ cup vinegar
1 teaspoon salt
2 cups boiling water
1 cup hot medium cream sauce

Cut off tops, wash, and scrape or lightly pare the salsify. Slice across into ½-inch thick slices; place into cold water with vinegar to prevent darkening. Drain and rinse in cold water. Add salt to boiling water. Add salsify, cover and cook about 20 to 25 minutes, or until soft but not broken. Drain; add cream sauce, mixing until blended. Serve as a vegetable. Makes 4 to 6 servings.

VEGETABLE STEW

- ½ cup butter or margarine
- 2 medium onions, chopped
- 1 clove garlic, minced
- 3 small green or yellow squash, scrubbed and cubed
- 2 raw ears fresh corn, or 1 cup canned kernel corn
- 2 small green peppers, diced
- 2 medium tomatoes, peeled and cubed
- 2 teaspoons salt
- Ground black pepper
- ¾ cup bouillon
- 2 tablespoons chopped parsley
- 1 tablespoon fresh lemon juice

Heat butter in large saucepan over moderate heat until frothy; add onions, garlic, and squash; cook 6 to 8 minutes, or until slightly brown, stirring frequently. Cut corn kernels off ears and add, together with peppers, tomatoes, salt, pepper, and bouillon. Lower heat. Cover and simmer 45 minutes, or until done. Add parsley and lemon juice at serving time. Makes 6 servings.

NOTE: One cup freshly shelled lima beans is a fine summer-time addition. When adding beans, the cooking time may be longer until beans are cooked. Other vegetables in season may be substituted.

BUTTERNUT SQUASH

- 3 lbs. butternut squash
- 1 cup cider or apple juice
- ¾ teaspoon salt
- 2 tablespoons butter or margarine
- ⅛ teaspoon ground black pepper

Pare squash and then cut open, discarding seeds and fibre. Cut squash into chips or thin slices. Place in small saucepan over moderate heat; add cider and salt. Cover and cook over low heat 25 to 30 minutes or until tender. Add butter and pepper. Mash until smooth. Makes 4 servings.

❧ HOPPING JOHN

1 lb. dry black-eyed peas, picked-over and washed
Cold water, to cover
2 bay leaves
1½ teaspoons salt
¼ teaspoon coarsely ground black pepper
¼ lb. salt pork, diced
1 large onion, chopped
3 cups hot cooked rice

Combine peas and cold water in saucepan. Add bay leaves, salt, and pepper. Cover and simmer 20 to 25 minutes. Meanwhile cook salt pork until crispy. Add onion and cook until golden, stirring constantly. Add to boiling peas; cover; and cook about 1 to 1¼ hours, or until tender. Serve hot cooked peas and broth over hot cooked rice. Makes 6 servings.

❧ KASHA

¼ cup butter or margarine
½ cup chopped onion
1 teaspoon whole celery seed
1 cup buckwheat groats
1 egg, beaten
2 cups hot water
1½ teaspoons salt

Heat butter in small saucepan. Add onion and celery seed; cook 5 to 6 minutes or until clear, but not colored. Mix together groats and egg. Add and cook, stirring constantly, 5 to 6 minutes or until dry. Add water and salt. Cover and cook over low heat 15 minutes, or until buckwheat groats are swelled and tender. Makes 4 servings.

☙ RED BEANS AND PINEAPPLE RICE

(One of Mrs. Louis Armstrong's favorite recipes)

1 lb. dry red kidney beans
½ lb. salt pork, diced
1 stalk celery, chopped
1 large onion, chopped
1 medium green pepper, diced
2 cloves garlic, crushed
1 tablespoon salt
1 teaspoon ground oregano
1 teaspoon ground basil leaves
2 bay leaves
3 to 4 whole cloves
3 dried red peppers
½ cup canned tomato sauce
1 cup raw, regular rice
1 cup chicken broth or bouillon
½ cup pineapple juice
¼ cup canned pineapple, crushed

Pick over, wash, and soak beans overnight in 8 cups lukewarm water. Next day, drain beans; place in large saucepan or kettle; add 1½ quarts cold water; bring to a boil over moderate heat. Meanwhile cook diced salt pork in frying pan or skillet until crispy; add celery, onion, and green pepper. Cook until soft, about 10 minutes. Skim froth off beans; add above vegetables, garlic, salt, oregano, ground basil, bay leaves, cloves, and red peppers. Cover and simmer until beans are almost tender, about 35 minutes; stir in tomato sauce and continue simmering until tender. Cook rice according to your own favorite recipe, using broth and pineapple juice as part of the usual amount of water. Add crushed pineapple to cooked drained rice and mix thoroughly. Serve beans with pineapple-rice as side dish. Makes 6 servings.

NOTE: Excellent with ham and other meats at a buffet party. Can be kept hot in server.

WHITE SAUCE

1 tablespoon butter or margarine
1 tablespoon flour
1 cup milk
½ teaspoon salt
Dash ground black pepper

Melt butter or margarine in small saucepan; remove from heat. Blend in flour, salt, and pepper; stir in milk slowly. Cook over low heat, stirring constantly, until sauce thickens and boils 1 minute. Serve hot. The measurements above are for a thin sauce. For medium sauce, use 2 tablespoons butter and flour; for thick sauce, use 3 tablespoons butter and flour. Makes 1 cup sauce.

NOTE: For smooth creamy white sauce, stir milk into flour-fat mixture very slowly while pan is away from heat; cook over low heat.

Variations

Cheddar-Cheese Sauce: Add ⅓ cup grated Cheddar cheese, ½ teaspoon Worcestershire sauce, and ¼ teaspoon paprika to 1 cup white sauce.

Horseradish Sauce: Add 1 tablespoon prepared horseradish and dash of nutmeg to 1 cup white sauce.

Stuffed Olive Sauce: Add ¼ cup chopped stuffed olives to 1 cup white sauce.

PARSNIPS YOU'LL RELISH

1½ lbs. parsnips
4 tablespoons butter or margarine
½ teaspoon salt
⅛ teaspoon sugar
5 to 6 wet outside lettuce leaves
2 tablespoons chopped parsley

Pare parsnips. Cut lengthwise into thin slices. Place butter in saucepan. Add parsnips, salt, and sugar. Cover completely with lettuce leaves. Cover and cook over low heat 18 to 20 minutes or until cooked and tender. Discard lettuce leaves. Sprinkle with parsley and serve. Makes 4 servings.

☙ OLD-FASHIONED ESCALLOPED ASPARAGUS

2 lbs. fresh asparagus
2 cups water
1 teaspoon salt
¼ cup butter or margarine
¼ cup flour
1 cup milk
½ cup asparagus liquid
½ teaspoon salt
1 teaspoon instant dried onion
8 crushed saltines
2 tablespoons melted butter or margarine
¼ teaspoon paprika

Break off and discard tough asparagus ends; remove scales from stalks; wash and cut 1½ inches off tip ends; set aside. Cut remaining stalks into 1-inch pieces; cook covered in boiling salted water 10 to 15 minutes or until tender; drain and set aside. Return liquid to saucepan; add asparagus tips. Cook, covered, 5 to 7 minutes or until tender but unbroken. Meanwhile, heat butter in small saucepan over moderate heat until frothy; stir in flour; gradually add milk, then asparagus liquid, stirring constantly. Add salt and onion; cook until thickened and smooth, stirring constantly. Remove from heat; add cooked asparagus bottoms. Mix until blended; turn into greased shallow casserole. Drain cooked tips; spread on top. Mix together saltines, butter, and paprika; sprinkle on top. Broil 2 to 3 minutes or until heated through and golden brown on top. Makes 4 to 5 servings.

4. *Fish*

WHY WE SHOULD EAT MORE FISH

Little do people realize that there are so many different kinds of fish from which to choose. The average home-maker's repertoire of fish to cook and serve runs something like this—fillet of sole or haddock, or flounder, smelts, cod fish, mackerel, halibut, salmon, bass, trout, swordfish, shad and bluefish, with slight regional variations from lakes and rivers in the area. Lucky indeed is the little woman who was taught by her mother, emigrated from across the ocean, to relish, for example, ray, shark, eel, catfish, ling, carp, monk-fish, barracuda, sturgeon, mullet or sea herring, and squid, to mention a few of the over 200 kinds of fish that are caught. Foreign sections of big cities have demand for varieties not sold in the supermarket. The supermarkets carry only those fish for which there is demand. If we un-derstood fish better, we'd eat more kinds and cook it with more affection.

What's so desirable about our eating more kinds of fish more often? With the exception of very few fish such as squid, devil fish, or abalone, well-cooked fish is tender and cooks quickly. There's always some kind of fish at the market that goes begging for buyers, at a reasonable price.

Fish turning up two or three times a week in the family menu adds variety to the daily meals. Fish is a main dish that stands alone for supplying the same high quality protein as meat. Also, the fish from the sea contain iodine and goodness knows what other traces of minerals from the sea to be uncovered in some future day, and to be of great value in our dietary needs. Fish is a natural food; the fish grew naturally and were not forced in any way to fatten for market.

Many fish varieties are available the year round, fresh or frozen. Buy fresh-caught fish as fillets and steaks, dressed or whole. Buy fresh-frozen fish for any other style.

Store frozen fish in freezer until just before thawing for cooking. Never refreeze it once it has thawed. Cook frozen fillets and steaks while frozen, proceeding as if they were thawed, but allowing more cooking time.

When thawing is necessary, thaw in refrigerator at 40 to 45°F. Thawing at room temperature causes too much dripping. To speed thawing, immerse the freezer-wrapped fish in cold running water.

Amount to Buy: Allow 1/3 to 1/2 lb. per person of edible part of whole fish; about 1 lb. per person of fish with head and tail, as purchased. Allow 1/3 lb. per person of fish fillets or steaks.

It's easy to learn how to cook fish.

Fish is baked.

Fish is broiled.

Fish is steamed, stewed, and boiled.

Fish is fried in deep fat.

Fish is fried or panned in a small amount of fat.

When one knows how to bake a whole bluefish, the same method applies to baking any whole fish; and broiling is the same for fish fillets, fish steaks, or fish halves of mackerel, cod, haddock, snapper, pollack, etc.

Never expect fish to brown, for fish contains little fat. Over-broiling fish in order to brown it only dries it out and never browns it satisfactorily. To brown fish, one must coat it with some ingredient or mixture with known browning qualities, such as eggs or egg yolks, buttered crumbs, cheese, heavy cream, or evaporated milk. The classic "browner" for fish to be broiled or baked a golden brown in the short time required to cook the fish till done is a fine mayonnaise. Mayonnaise is a rich emulsion of oil and eggs and egg yolk with a spicy bonus to add savor to the cooked fish. Mayonnaise browns with rich tempting tones very quickly under broiler heat. So brush your fish liberally with mayonnaise before broiling; broil as usual—but you won't have to cook as long till it looks and is done. The results will astound you. Add grated cheese, spices, or condiments; baste with wine, melted butter, or oil during broiling; add lemon juice after broiling; add chopped parsley after broiling.

Fish is bland in flavor and needs rich sauces and peppy seasonings. In fact, as the seasoning combinations vary, so vary the resultant dishes. When in doubt as to the accompaniment, serve the usual lemon or tartare sauce; accompany with tart-flavored salads, cucumber, pickles, etc.

Before pan-cooking fish, the fish should be rolled in some sort of coating that browns easily, such as flour or corn meal; it may be dipped in a batter; it may be dipped in beaten egg diluted slightly with milk or water, then in flour or in fine crumbs. This applies to fish fillets, fish steaks, or any small whole fish such as smelts, whiting, porgies, sea trout, or bass, etc.

When some fish unknown to you is selling plentifully and at a good price, give it a try. When whiting is running, it often sells at very low prices and yet goes begging. Even if you've never cooked whiting before, cook it by any method you'd cook sea bass or fillet of any fish. You could fry it or pan cook it in a little fat. You can broil it, following the same method you would for fillet or a slice of halibut.

Another argument for fish that should make the guardian of the family's health serve her family more fish comes specifically from Dr. Norman Jolliffe, Director of the Bureau of Nutrition, New York City Department of Health, who recommends that for a longer and healthier life we would do well to take a page from the Japanese, Bantu, and Italian Dietary and eat fish four times a week.

Generally today, with quick freezing and our streamlined refrigeration, the problem of "not-fresh" or "smelly" fish is practically non-existent.

INSTRUCTIONS FOR PREPARING LOBSTERS

It never fails . . . after we have a show featuring live lobsters, both phone calls and mail bring in questions such as this: "Dear Josie . . . My husband brought home live lobsters for me to broil. Should I boil them first, then broil them? Where do I start?"

This is a typical phone call. (Yes, I get questions by phone as well as by mail.) "My mother thought she was doing me a favor by not having me help her with the cooking. Now I wish I'd been more interested and helped her anyhow. It's most puzzling when some specialty dish like lobster confronts me. I have no experience to fall back on." *Rewarding* is a word hardly expressive enough to tell you the outcome of these little chats. A week or so later a letter will tell how delicious the lobster was . . . and go on to say "that from now on, fixing lobster is no problem at all."

The main question is "How do I open then clean the lobster?" Here's how, in brief: First collect a big cutting board, a small sharp knife, a heavy knife slightly longer than the full length of the straightened lobster, and a heavy wooden mallet (I use the rolling pin). Place the lobster on the board. Insert the point of the small, sharp knife in the true center between the body shell and the first tail segment. Cut about ½ inch in that spot, not clear across. This breaks the spinal cord and kills the lobster at once. Turn it on its back. Then place the big knife cutting side down along the center of the full length of the lobster. Grasp the knife handle firmly; then, using the other hand, hit all along the blunt edge of the knife with the wooden mallet or rolling pin until the knife cuts through the undershell and meat, just through to the hard shell. Spread the lobster open and the undershell will crack evenly all the way with gentle pressure so that the lobster will lie flat; do not pull apart. Remove the vein you'll find running through the center of the tail segment. Remove the small irregular parchment-like sac about 2 inches long, sometimes called the "lady," that is in the body cavity, just below the head. Remove the finger-like gills just above the tail meat. This is all that need be discarded. The soft green material is the liver and it is rich and delicious and my favorite eating. The coral is also edible, nutritious, and tasty. Crack the large claws with a hammer or mallet, leaving them attached. When liver is present, I scoop it out and mix it with buttered bread crumbs, a little chopped parsley, and onion;

spice it highly with tabasco, salt, and pepper; and then I fill the body cavity with this before broiling. It makes a good extender and goes well with the broiled lobster meat.

"To broil lobster?" Simple as can be. Brush the meaty side of the lobster with plenty of melted butter or margarine; sprinkle with salt and pepper. Broil 3 inches from heat, in a pre-heated broiler, fleshy side up, about 12 to 16 minutes (depending on size), or until done but not dried out, brushing with melted butter three or four times; do not turn. Serve at once with melted butter or margarine on the side, and lemon wedges.

☙ CURRIED LOBSTER IN THE SHELL

2 (2 lbs. each) boiled lobsters
¼ cup butter or margarine
2 teaspoons curry powder
2 cups chopped fresh whole mushrooms
1 small clove garlic, minced
3 tablespoons flour
1½ cups light cream
¼ cup sherry wine
3 egg yolks, well beaten
1 teaspoon salt
½ cup cracker crumbs
2 to 3 tablespoons melted butter or margarine
Diced cucumbers, sliced radishes, and lemon

Split cooked lobsters lengthwise in half; remove and discard the veins and sacs near heads. Remove body meat. reserving the shells. Break the claws and pick out all meat. Dice lobster meat fine; set aside. Meanwhile, melt butter in large skillet or frying pan. Add curry, mushrooms, and garlic. Cook about 10 to 12 minutes, or until dry, stirring occasionally. Stir in flour; gradually add cream, stirring until slightly thickened. Add sherry and blend. Stir about ½ cup of the hot mixture into egg yolks. Return to mixture in pan and cook about 2 to 3 minutes, stirring constantly.

Remove from heat. Add lobster meat and salt. Mix well; spoon the mixture into shells. Sprinkle with cracker crumbs blended with butter. Bake in a moderate oven (350°F.) about 15 minutes or until lightly browned. Serve with diced cucumbers, sliced radishes, and lemon. Makes 4 servings.

☙ LOBSTER AND SHRIMP IN THE SHELL

1 tablespoon butter or margarine
1 tablespoon chopped onion
1 tablespoon chopped green pepper
2 tablespoons all-purpose flour
¼ teaspoon salt
⅛ teaspoon ground black pepper
½ teaspoon curry powder
1 chicken bouillon cube
½ cup boiling water
½ cup heavy cream
2 boiled lobsters (1½ lbs. each)
½ lb. shrimp, cooked, peeled, deveined, and diced
½ cup soft bread crumbs
2 tablespoons melted butter or margarine

Heat butter in saucepan over moderate heat until frothy; add onion and green pepper; cook 5 minutes or until soft, stirring constantly. Add flour, salt, pepper, and curry powder, stirring until blended. Dissolve bouillon cube in boiling water; gradually add to onion mixture, stirring constantly. Cook 5 minutes, stirring frequently; gradually add cream, stirring constantly until thoroughly heated but not boiling; remove from heat and set aside. Split lobsters in half; discard vein and the sac at top of body cavity. Lift out lobster meat; crack claws; remove and dice the meat. Stir diced lobster and shrimp into set-aside sauce. Fill lobster shells with lobster-shrimp mixture. Mix together bread crumbs and melted butter; sprinkle over filled lobsters. Bake in moderate oven (375°F.) about 15 minutes or until done. Makes 4 servings.

◆ LOBSTER TAILS FRA DIAVOLO

2 to 3 (4 to 5 oz.) frozen rock lobster tails
1 clove garlic, minced
½ teaspoon salt
3 tablespoons olive oil
½ teaspoon crushed red pepper
1 teaspoon whole oregano leaves, crumbled
1 can (8 oz.) tomato sauce
2 tablespoons brandy
2 tablespoons minced parsley

Remove meat from lobster shells; cut into 1½-inch pieces. Place garlic and salt in large skillet or frying pan over moderate heat; crush and mash garlic fine. Add oil, red pepper, oregano, and tomato sauce. Cook uncovered over high heat about 5 to 6 minutes, or until thickened, stirring occasionally. Add lobster meat; lower heat; cook about 10 minutes or until firm and opaque, stirring frequently. Remove from heat. Warm the brandy in large spoon; hold lighted match directly over it until it flames; pour brandy over lobster and sauce. Stir until flames are extinguished. Sprinkle with minced parsley. This is a perfect dish to make at the table in your electric skillet in full view of the diners. Makes 4 servings.

◆ FRIED RICE WITH CRAB MEAT

This is a delicious dish—and so simple I'm afraid that you'll feel like I do. I hate to take credit for it because it's almost no work at all. You can put this together at the last minute, and give the impression that you're a finished cook. All this recipe requires is to find the ingredients and put them in a frying pan. Let them get really hot. Marvelous what you can do in a frying pan when you want to. This is a great Lenten dish—a great Friday dish if you're not eating meat.

- 2 eggs, beaten
- 1½ teaspoons salt
- ⅛ teaspoon ground black pepper
- 2 tablespoons salad oil
- ¼ cup minced onion
- ¼ cup minced celery
- ½ cup sliced canned mushrooms, drained
- 1 can (6½ oz.) crab meat, flaked
- 4 cups hot cooked rice
- 2 tablespoons soy sauce

Mix together eggs, salt, and pepper in bowl. Heat oil in large skillet or frying pan over moderate heat and pour in mixture. Cook without stirring until set and lightly browned underneath. Working quickly and in the pan, cut across thin pancake with 2 knives to shred into small pieces. Push shredded eggs to one side of pan. Cook onion and celery in cleared space about 2 minutes or until heated through. Add mushrooms, crab meat, rice, and soy sauce. Heat thoroughly, stirring constantly. Makes 4 servings.

☙ DEVILED CRAB

Deviled crab should be spicy, crusty brown, piping hot, and fragrant. I think you'll find the combination of curry powder, lime juice, parsley, celery, and green pepper adds spiciness. You'll rejoice when you poke the crab's brown crust, to be greeted by rich smelling steam, and real crab meat, not a substitute filler. You'll appreciate the little trick of masking the molded crab with rich mayonnaise before baking in order to give it a tempting brown crust.

Now about the tartare sauce. There are more recipes for making tartare sauce than you could shake a stick at—but I think we all agree that it begins with mayonnaise. There's no rule of thumb about what to add and how much.

Chopped peppers, pimientos, olives, capers, chives, onion, parsley, sour pickles, tarragon, wine vinegar, lemon or lime juice, even finely diced avocado pear make up the list from which to select what to add to the mayonnaise to make tartare sauce. There are undoubtedly other regional condiments used that are not mentioned here.

1½ cups flaked fresh or canned crab meat
3 slices fresh white bread, crumbled
2 tablespoons minced parsley
2 tablespoons minced green pepper
½ cup minced celery
1 cup undiluted canned cream of mushroom soup
½ teaspoon salt
Few drops bottled hot sauce
1 tablespoon curry powder
1 tablespoon fresh lime or lemon juice
½ cup mayonnaise
½ cup fine dry bread crumbs
Paprika

Mix together crab meat, bread, parsley, green pepper, celery, soup, salt, hot sauce, curry powder, and lime juice. Spoon into six greased individual casseroles or crab shells. Round tops of mixture and spread evenly with mayonnaise. Pat crumbs onto mayonnaise. Sprinkle with paprika. Bake uncovered in a hot oven (400°F.) about ½ hour or until piping hot throughout and browned. Serve with tartare sauce. Makes 6 servings.

SHRIMP IN PACKET

½ lb. cream cheese
½ lb. Roquefort cheese
4 chopped pimientos
1 lb. raw shrimp, shelled and deveined
4 slices lemon
4 squares (12-inch) aluminum foil or greased heavy brown paper

Mix together cheese and pimientos. Mash into smooth paste. Spread mixture evenly to within ½ inch of edges of foil squares. Place shrimp in center; top with sliced lemon. Close by pinching tops together. Place in shallow baking pan; bake in a hot oven (400°F.) 30 minutes, or until done. To serve, place each hot packet on a plate and let each guest open his own. Makes 4 servings.

SHRIMP GUMBO

You've never tasted a gumbo until you've tasted this! I almost speak reverently about this dish because I consider it one of my masterpieces. This is my own personal recipe. Yes, I ate something like this many years ago, but I never asked for the recipe. I just ad-libbed it together. I didn't want to lose one speck of the shrimp flavor—notice I even boil the shells and use that stock for the broth of the soup. Oh my, this is good! I feel just a little bit jealous about this recipe. I hope if you do use it you won't change it one bit—make it just this way—add, maybe, a little salt. You know how some commercials are on TV—with a money-back guarantee; well, I feel like saying that if you don't go for this "you'll get your money back."

- ¾ to 1 lb. raw shrimp
- 3 cups water
- 2 teaspoons salt
- 2 tablespoons butter or margarine
- 1 clove garlic, minced
- 1 large onion, chopped
- 1 large green pepper, diced
- 2 cups canned tomatoes
- 2 cups canned or sliced fresh okra
- ¼ teaspoon ground black pepper
- ½ teaspoon ground basil leaves
- 1 teaspoon sugar
- 2 tablespoons chopped parsley
- 1½ cups hot cooked rice

Wash, peel, devein, and dice shrimp. Set aside in refrigerator. Save shrimp shells and rinse in cold water. Combine shells, water, and salt in medium kettle. Cover and simmer about 20 minutes. Melt butter in skillet or frying pan over moderate heat. Add garlic, onion, and green pepper; cook about 10 minutes, stirring frequently. Strain and reserve broth from shells. Discard shells; return broth to kettle. Add garlic, onion, and green pepper mixture, the tomatoes and raw okra. If okra is canned, do not add yet. Cover and simmer about ½ hour. Add ground pepper, ground basil, sugar, diced shrimp, and canned okra (if raw okra was not used). Cover and simmer about 10 minutes. Add parsley. Serve gumbo in shallow soup plates. Spoon hot rice into each serving. This makes approximately 2 quarts gumbo, or 6 to 8 servings.

SHRIMP IN YOUR BEER

To read this recipe you would believe that we had taken leave of our senses. Imagine serving unpeeled and undeveined or not fully cleaned shrimp on the table. It's just one of those things—and makes the biggest hit ever! I'll never forget about two years ago, when an advertising and promotion manager of an agency that handles a big supermarket chain called me and said, "Josie, will you please make an appearance next Friday afternoon at the opening of our Spring Valley store and after that come on over to my house just across the Hudson River and we'll have a party at my house. We'll call up the Hudson Valley Amateur Theatre Group and they'll join us and we'll really have a bang-up time. What do you suggest that we eat?" "Oh, don't worry about that," I said, "we'll serve shrimp and baked potatoes." "What'll I get?" he asked. I said, "Well, I'll bring up about 10 or 15 pounds of jumbo shrimp. You just get plenty of Idaho potatoes for baking and get enough fixings for a big tossed salad—all the greens you can get your hands on—or tell your wife to put them in." By the time we got to Ossining via Bear Mountain the Hudson Valley group was there—about half of them. "Show me to the kitchen" says I, because we were lugging the load of shrimp. They were quick-frozen and had been refrigerating themselves all along the trip home and thawing obligingly at the same time. Some of the women followed me in with "what can I do—can I help?" You know how folks ask that when you're preparing dinner and they come in before you're through—they all want to help. So I said, "Sure you can." I told one to peel potatoes, told two or three more to get busy on the salad greens, and I got to the shrimp and the potatoes. And this is what I did. I cut the big peeled potatoes into thin slices, then sliced them across to make match-like strips. I rounded up all the frying pans in the house (fortunately I had remembered to tell the host to have his wife put in plenty of butter), and I put the potatoes to cook pancake style in butter. You'll find the recipe under Swiss potatoes. They're always very well accepted. Then I called for the biggest saucepans and kettle, Dutch oven, anything big short of a wash boiler (and would have used that if they didn't have anything else). But I did get the pots out and just washed the shrimp and put them in with the ingredients that you see below. Meanwhile the potatoes got ready to turn over and we turned those over upside down on a big plate and put them back into the pan. They were just beautiful. They had a brown crust on top, and we let them cook until they had a brown crust underneath. The salad greens were ready by then; and we tossed these with good sharp vinegar, oil, and a little garlic as dressing. And I turned the shrimp into a great big old-fashioned antique wash basin. We had plenty of French bread, which was heated till crisp in the oven—and I want to tell you that if you ever go through Ossining and you talk to any member of the Hudson Valley Amateur Players Group, they will tell you that this was the most delicious feed they ever remembered.

Do you know it didn't take more than an hour from the time I walked in the door till we had it on the table. Of course, many hands make light work. They did do the K.P. on the potatoes and on the salad greens. You can see that for a gang this is a perfect dish because there's so little preparation, no technique, no particular skill needed—just a little watching and a little daring in order to try it on guests. Nobody seems to mind having to peel his own shrimp. Of course, I had great big ones—three or four shrimp were as big as your fist. I think that the secret of this dish is to get the biggest shrimp you can get your hands on—even if you have to order them ahead of time, and you can always do that when you're planning on a party.

2 lbs. raw, unpeeled, jumbo shrimp, washed
1 sliced onion
½ teaspoon whole caraway seed
2 cloves garlic, crushed
¼ teaspoon curry powder
2 sprigs parsley, coarsely chopped
2 celery tops, chopped
½ teaspoon coarsely ground black pepper
¾ tablespoon coarse or sea salt
1 to 1½ cups beer
Melted butter or margarine

Place shrimp in large saucepan. Add onion, caraway seed, garlic, curry powder, parsley, celery, pepper, salt, and beer. Cover tightly and place over high heat. When steam forms, cook 3 minutes. Stir well. Cover and cook about 2 to 3 minutes longer, or until shrimp are cooked. When shrimp have turned pink they are done. Drain shrimp; serve piping hot and unpeeled. Serve unstrained broth in bowls. Serve melted butter in small butter dunking dishes. Makes 4 servings.

NOTE: Pass dampened warm napkins or paper towels for fingers with this—since each diner peels his own shrimp.

◆§ LEMON SCAMPI

2 lbs. fresh or frozen shrimp
¼ cup butter or margarine
2 cloves garlic, minced
Juice of 1 lemon
¼ cup melted butter or margarine
Salt and ground white pepper to taste
Chopped parsley

Remove shells from shrimp, except for the portion that covers the tail. Cut down center of back; remove sand vein and rinse shrimp quickly. Melt butter in small skillet or frying pan over moderate heat. Add garlic and lemon juice. Simmer 3 minutes, stirring often. Place shrimp on individual flame-proof platters or broiling pan lined with foil to save washing. Add melted butter to garlic; blend; pour over shrimp. Sprinkle with salt and pepper. Place in pre-heated broiler 4 inches from heat. Broil about 5 to 7 minutes, turning once, or until lightly browned. Sprinkle with chopped parsley. Serve at once with all pan juices. Makes 4 servings.

◆§ ESCARGOTS (SNAILS) IN GARLIC AND PARSLEY BUTTER SAUCE

36 snails and shells (allow 6 snails per portion—buy the combination package of cleaned prepared shells and cooked canned snails)
½ cup butter or margarine, at room temperature
3 cloves garlic, minced
2 medium shallots, minced
¼ cup finely chopped parsley
½ teaspoon salt
⅛ teaspoon ground pepper
⅛ teaspoon (scant) nutmeg
Crusty French bread

Drain and rinse canned snails, discarding the liquid. Mix together in a bowl butter, garlic, shallots, parsley, salt, pepper, and nutmeg, beating until creamy. Pack inner coils of snail shells with butter mixture leaving room enough for the snails. Push snails into shells and fill shells with remaining butter mixture, sealing the openings. Chill ½ hour or longer before baking. Place filled snails in hollows of special snail dishes; bake in a hot oven (400°F.) 15 minutes or until butter and juices boil in dish. Serve bubbling hot, with snail holders and snail picks. Pass French bread to sop up butter and juices that are in the pan and get poured out of the shell by the diner. Makes 6 servings.

SAVORY STEAMED MUSSELS

- 1½ quarts (3½–4 doz.) mussels
- ¼ cup olive oil
- 2 cloves garlic, crushed
- 1 cup dry white wine
- 2 to 3 dried red peppers, crumbled
- 1 teaspoon whole oregano leaves, crumbled
- 3 to 4 whole scallions, chopped
- 2 tablespoons chopped parsley
- Sliced crisp French or Italian bread

Scrub shells of mussels; scrape away all beard; wash and rinse thoroughly. Place olive oil and garlic in large saucepan over moderate heat. Add cleaned mussels, wine, red peppers, oregano, and scallions. Cover and cook 8 to 10 minutes or until all the mussels have opened. Lift top shells off mussels and discard. Sprinkle parsley on top. Place one to two slices of bread in deep soup plates. Spoon mussels and broth over bread. Provide side dishes for emptied shells. Makes 4 servings.

◆ PANNED SCALLOPS WITH HERBS

1½ lbs. scallops
⅓ cup flour
½ teaspoon salt
⅛ teaspoon ground white pepper
⅓ cup olive oil
2 tablespoons sliced scallions
1 clove garlic, minced
½ teaspoon ground thyme leaves
¼ cup chopped parsley
2 tablespoons fresh lemon juice
6 slices hot buttered toast

Do not wash scallops. Pat scallops with absorbent paper. Mix together flour, salt, and pepper. Roll scallops in mixture. Heat oil in large skillet or frying pan over high heat. Add scallops; cook about 6 to 7 minutes or until lightly browned, turning repeatedly. Add scallions, garlic, and thyme; cook about 2 to 3 minutes longer, stirring constantly. Add parsley and lemon juice; stir well; remove from heat; spoon scallops and pan juices onto hot buttered toast. Makes 6 servings.

◆ CLAM PATTIES

1 can (7 oz.) minced clams
¼ cup clam liquid
½ cup cracker crumbs
1 egg, beaten
1 tablespoon chopped onion
2 tablespoons fresh lemon juice
1 cup fat for shallow frying

Drain clams, reserving ¼ cup of the liquid. Mix together clams, ¼ cup liquid, cracker crumbs, egg, onion, and lemon juice. Heat fat in skillet or frying pan over medium heat. Drop clam mixture by tablespoons into the hot fat. Fry quickly, turning to brown both sides. Serve with catsup, chili sauce, tartare sauce, or lemon wedges. Makes 6 patties.

☙ BAKED CHERRYSTONE CLAMS IN THE SHELL

Aluminum foil
6 to 9 cherrystone clams, opened on the half shell
3 tablespoons soft butter or margarine
½ teaspoon anchovy paste
1 teaspoon finely chopped parsley
2 slices bacon, diced
1 tablespoon chopped pimiento

Crinkle and crush aluminum foil and place deep enough to steady the clams in shallow baking-serving dish or pie pan. Arrange clams in shells in foil creases, taking care juice does not spill into pan. Mix together butter, anchovy paste, and parsley. Spread mixture over clams. Sprinkle bacon and pimiento on top. Broil 3 inches from heat in pre-heated broiler 4 to 5 minutes or until done. Serve from baking dish. Makes 1 serving.

☙ BAKED CLAMS WITH RICE

4 tablespoons butter or margarine
4 tablespoons flour
½ teaspoon salt
⅛ teaspoon ground black pepper
2 cups hot milk
½ cup thick tomato paste
1 dozen shucked large cherrystone clams, chopped
4 cups cooked rice
¼ cup soft bread crumbs
2 tablespoons melted butter or margarine
2 tablespoons grated American cheese

Melt butter in small saucepan over low heat. Add flour, salt, and pepper. Stir until blended; cook until frothy. Gradually add milk, stirring constantly. Cook, stirring frequently until thickened and smooth. Remove from heat;

add tomato paste and clams with their juice. Blend. Arrange alternate layers of rice and clam mixture in greased, shallow medium, casserole. Mix together bread crumbs, melted butter, and cheese. Sprinkle on top. Bake uncovered in hot oven (400°F.) about 20 minutes or until bubbly and browned. Makes 6 servings.

SEA FOOD PAELLA

¼ cup olive oil or salad oil
1 large onion, chopped
2 cloves garlic, minced
1½ cups raw regular rice
3 cups water
4 frozen rock lobster tails
½ lb. raw shrimp
1½ to 2 teaspoons salt
Few drops Tabasco
½ teaspoon ground saffron
½ pint (1 cup) raw shucked oysters or clams with juice
1 cup hot cooked peas
4 canned pimiento pods, cut into strips
2 tablespoons chopped parsley
½ cup ripe olives

Heat oil in large kettle or saucepan over moderate heat. Add onion, garlic, and rice. Cook about 6 to 8 minutes until straw-colored, stirring constantly. Add water; cover and simmer 15 minutes. Meanwhile, cut lobster tails in chunks cross-wise through shell. Peel and devein shrimp. Add seasonings, lobster in shell, shrimp, and oysters to above. Cover and simmer until rice is tender, about 15 to 20 minutes. Spoon onto heated serving platter. Place peas around the edge and arrange pimiento in the center. Sprinkle with chopped parsley. Garnish with olives. Makes 6 servings.

Paella is often made with both meat and seafood. Cooked cubed veal, pork, or chicken may be added at the same time as the shellfish. In this case meat broth from cooking the meat may be used instead of all or part of the three cups water.

PORTUGUESE FISH FILLET CASSEROLE
(Pascado Costa Brave)

- 12 to 16 potato balls or pared tiny new potatoes
- 1⅓ lb. fish fillets (flounder or haddock), fresh or frozen
- 1½ tablespoons fresh lemon juice
- 1 teaspoon salt
- ¾ teaspoon ground black pepper
- ½ cup flour
- ½ cup olive or salad oil
- 1 clove garlic
- 2 small onions, chopped
- 2 tablespoons minced parsley
- 1 can (8½ oz.) peas and liquid
- 2 tablespoons melted butter or margarine

Cook potatoes in boiling salted water to cover, about 8 to 10 minutes or until tender. Drain and set aside. Cut fish into serving pieces. Sprinkle with lemon juice, salt, and pepper. Coat with flour. Heat oil in large skillet or frying pan over moderate heat. Add garlic and cook about 3 minutes or until faintly colored. Remove garlic and discard. Add fish and cook about 3 minutes on each side. Transfer fish to four individual casseroles. Combine onions, parsley, and peas and blend. Spread over fish. Arrange cooked potatoes around fish. Dribble melted butter on top. Bake in a hot oven (400°F.) about 15 minutes until fish flakes easily when tested with a fork. Serve at once. Makes 4 servings.

BAKED SEA BASS SEBASTIAN

- 4 (1 lb. each) whole sea bass, dressed
- Salt and ground black pepper
- 1 cup mayonnaise or salad dressing
- 1 cup finely crushed corn flakes or shredded wheat

Rinse and wipe fish dry. Season entire insides with salt and pepper. Spread mayonnaise evenly over entire outside of fish. Coat with crushed cereal. Place fish 1 to 1½ inches apart in ungreased shallow pan (line pan with foil to save washing). Bake in a hot oven (425°F.) about 35 to 40 minutes or until fish flakes away from bones on testing with fork. Serve with baked potatoes and Snappy Cole Slaw (page 186). Makes 4 servings.

FISH FILLETS THERMIDOR

Here again is another way to glamorize fish fillets. Notice I use mayonnaise a lot with fish fillets—it always does a good job. It adds the flavor and the richness that lean fish lacks; Parmesan cheese adds flavor too. You'll enjoy this a lot. You'll find oodles of recipes for meats, pies, cakes, and vegetables, but recipes for fish which the family really likes are rather few and far between. Treasure this one, please, because it is bound to be a favorite, and it will always be eaten up to the last bite.

- ¾ cup milk
- 1 cup mayonnaise or salad dressing
- ¾ cup canned sliced mushrooms and liquid
- ¼ cup sherry
- 1½ lbs. fish fillets, fresh or frozen
- ¾ teaspoon salt
- ¼ teaspoon ground black pepper
- ¼ cup soft bread crumbs
- ½ cup grated Parmesan cheese
- ¼ teaspoon paprika
- 2 tablespoons melted butter or margarine

Stir milk into mayonnaise; whip until smooth. Add mushrooms and sherry; mix well. Spread ½ of the sauce on bottom of greased shallow baking dish. Sprinkle fish with salt and pepper; place over sauce. Cover with remaining sauce. Mix together bread crumbs, cheese, paprika, and melted butter. Sprinkle on top. Bake uncovered in moderate oven

(375°F.) about 25 to 35 minutes, or until fish flakes easily when tested with fork. Makes 4 servings.

NOTE: Fillets of cod, haddock, flounder, or sole may be used.

BROILED SHAD ROE WITH BACON ON TOAST

Shad roe is delectable eating and commands a fancy price in fine restaurants. There's a little trick to broiling this delicacy. If the heat goes too high, the protective membrane splits and the roe flies out and makes a mess in the oven. To avoid any such disaster, the restaurant and hotel chefs have devised the method of first poaching the roes in a spicy broth until they "set." Then they oil and broil them. Now that's all very well as to results, but the taste is so altered by this practice that the little extra precaution of broiling gently is nothing when you consider how much better the finished roes will taste. If your broiler only has one heat, and you can't keep the heat low, you can get good results by controlling the distance from the heat source. The whole idea is that the roes must cook slowly through to the center without bursting.

3 pairs shad roe
1 teaspoon salt
⅛ teaspoon ground white pepper
¼ cup salad oil
6 slices hot buttered toast
¼ cup hot melted butter or margarine
2 tablespoons fresh lemon juice
2 tablespoons chopped parsley
6 slices crisp bacon
Lemon wedges

Gently separate roes if attached; wipe with damp cloth; do not break delicate protective membrane. Place roes side by side in shallow dish; sprinkle with salt and pepper; brush generously on both sides with oil. Let stand at room temperature about 25 minutes. Pre-heat broiler about 5 minutes; place roes on greased broiler rack; broil 6 to 7 inches from heat about 7 to 8 minutes; turn; brush with oil; broil about 6 to 7 minutes or until done but not burst open. Place roes on toast. Mix together butter, lemon juice, and parsley; pour over roes. Top with crisp bacon. Garnish with lemon. Makes 6 servings.

POPPY CANNON'S PORTUGUESE STUFFED FLOUNDER FILLETS

2 whole flounder fillets
Salt and ground black pepper
1 tablespoon olive oil
1 onion, sliced
½ cup chopped cooked ham, bacon, or Cheddar cheese
2 egg yolks
1 tablespoon melted butter
½ cup soft bread crumbs
Paprika
2 tablespoons Port wine
1 tablespoon fresh lemon juice
2 cups mashed potatoes
Sliced lemon for garnish

Season fish with salt and pepper. Place oil and onions in shallow baking-serving dish. Lay one fillet over onions; spread with ham, bacon, or cheese. Cover with remaining fillet. Mix together egg yolks and butter; spread over fish. Sprinkle bread crumbs and paprika on top. Sprinkle with wine and lemon juice. Season mashed potatoes with salt and pepper; arrange in a border around fish. Bake in a hot (425°F.) oven 25–30 minutes or until fish is cooked. Garnish with sliced lemon. Makes 5 to 6 servings.

SWEET AND SOUR PIKE

1 (3-3½ lbs.) whole fresh pike, dressed
½ cup brown sugar
½ cup cider vinegar
1 medium onion, sliced
2 to 3 teaspoons salt
3 cups boiling water
¼ cup raisins
¼ cup blanched sliced almonds
4 gingersnaps, crumbled fine
Additional salt, brown sugar, vinegar, to taste

Wash and drain fish; cut across into 2 to 2½-inch steaks; set aside. Remove gills and eyes from head; wash head well. Place fish and head into large skillet. Add brown sugar, vinegar, onion, and salt. Cover with boiling water. Place over moderate heat; cover and simmer 15 to 18 minutes or until fish flakes on testing with fork. Lift out fish slices only; place in deep serving dish. Strain broth; pour into saucepan over moderate heat; add raisins and almonds. Mix together gingersnaps and ½ cup of the hot fish stock; return to boiling mixture, stirring until smooth. Add more salt, brown sugar, and vinegar to taste. Pour over fish. Cool and chill until jellied. Makes 4 to 6 servings.

BROILED BLUEFISH

- 1 (3 to 3½ lbs.) bluefish, dressed
- ½ cup melted butter or margarine
- ¼ teaspoon paprika
- 1 teaspoon seasoned salt
- ⅛ teaspoon ground black pepper
- ½ teaspoon ground basil leaves
- 1 tablespoon fresh lemon juice
- 1 tablespoon chopped parsley

Have fish split for broiling and cut into 6 equal portions. Pre-heat broiler about 10 minutes. Wash and pat fish dry with absorbent paper; place skin-side up on greased broiler rack. Broil 4 inches from heat about 8 minutes or until skin is crispy. Turn and brush with melted butter. Sprinkle with paprika. Continue broiling about 5 minutes, or until done. Mix together remaining butter, salt, pepper, basil, and lemon juice; spread mixture over fish; broil about 1 minute. Place on heated platter. Sprinkle with parsley. Makes 6 servings.

◆§ BAKED HALIBUT CREOLE

¼ cup butter or margarine
1 large onion, chopped
⅓ green pepper, diced
1 clove garlic, minced
1½ cups canned tomatoes
½ cup sliced fresh or canned mushrooms
1 teaspoon salt
⅛ teaspoon cayenne pepper
4 portion-sized halibut steaks, fresh or frozen
Chopped parsley

Heat butter in large skillet or frying pan over moderate heat. Add onion, green pepper, and garlic. Cook 4 minutes or until soft, stirring frequently. Add tomatoes, mushrooms, salt, and pepper. Cover and simmer 15 minutes. Arrange halibut in greased shallow baking dish. Pour hot sauce over fish. Bake uncovered in hot oven (425°F.) 25 to 30 minutes or until done upon testing. To test, gently pierce fish with fork; when fish flesh flakes easily, it is done. Remove from oven. Sprinkle parsley on top. Makes 4 servings.

◆§ FISH TERIYAKI

⅓ cup soy sauce
⅓ cup saki or sherry wine
1 clove garlic, crushed
8 to 12 butterfish or smelts, dressed
Bamboo skewers

Mix together soy sauce, wine, and garlic; pour over fish in shallow dish. Refrigerate 3 hours or longer, turning fish over in sauce 2 or 3 times. To cook, spear a pair of fish onto 2 skewers as follows: Drain fish, reserving sauce; force one skewer through heads of two fish; force another skewer through thick tail parts of same pair. Push fish ½ inch apart. Broil 3 inches from broiler heat 3 to 4 minutes on each side, or until done, turning over once and basting 2 to 3 times with reserved sauce. Excellent and dramatic to cook before family or guests on outdoor grill. Makes 4 servings (2 to 3 fish per serving).

BAKED STUFFED RED SNAPPER

- 1 (4 to 5 lbs.) whole red snapper, dressed
- Salt and ground black pepper
- 1½ cups soft bread crumbs
- ¼ cup finely chopped onion
- ½ cup finely chopped celery leaves
- ¼ cup finely chopped parsley
- 3 tablespoons oil
- 1 teaspoon salt
- ¼ teaspoon ground black pepper
- 1 egg, beaten
- ¼ cup milk
- Oil
- Lemon wedges
- Crisp watercress

Wash, drain, and pat fish dry. Salt and pepper inside of fish. Mix together bread crumbs, onion, celery leaves, parsley, oil, salt, pepper, egg, and milk until blended. Stuff into fish; skewer and lace closed. Slash top of fish skin, making 3 equidistant slashes to keep skin from bursting during baking. Place fish on greased heavy brown paper or aluminum foil in open baking pan; brush fish with oil. Bake uncovered, in moderate oven (400°F.), 50 to 55 minutes or until done. Fish is done if flesh flakes when tested with fork. Lift out fish on paper or foil; transfer to warmed serving platter, gently pushing fish from paper onto platter. Serve garnished with lemon wedges and watercress. Makes 6 servings.

BAKED BLUEFISH, TOMATO SAUCE

2 cups soft bread crumbs, lightly packed
½ cup chopped celery leaves
2 tablespoons grated onion
2 tablespoons melted butter or margarine
½ teaspoon salt
⅛ teaspoon ground black pepper
¼ teaspoon ground sage leaves
¼ cup boiling water
1 (3 to 4 lbs.) whole bluefish, dressed
Salt and ground black pepper
Melted butter or margarine

Mix together bread crumbs, celery, onion, butter, salt, pepper, sage, and boiling water until dressing forms; set aside. Wash and drain bluefish; pat dry. Lightly season with salt and pepper on inside. Stuff with dressing; do not close opening. Place into greased baking-serving dish; brush with melted butter. Bake uncovered in hot oven (500°F.) 15 minutes; reduce oven heat to moderate (400°F.) and bake 25 to 30 minutes or until fish flakes easily upon testing with a fork.

Tomato Sauce for Bluefish

2 tablespoons olive oil or butter or margarine
2 tablespoons minced celery
2 tablespoons minced onion
1 tablespoon flour
1 cup tomato juice
1 teaspoon salt
1 tablespoon brown sugar
2 to 3 whole cloves

Heat oil in small saucepan over moderate heat until hot but not smoking; add celery and onion; cook, stirring constantly until beginning to brown. Add flour; cook 1 minute. Gradually add tomato juice, stirring constantly. Add salt, sugar, and cloves. Cover and simmer 10 minutes.

Strain; pour over baked fish in baking dish. Serve fish from baking dish. Makes 4 servings.

NOTE: Tomato sauce can be prepared while fish is baking.

☙ TUNA PATTIES WITH SPAGHETTI

2 cans (7 oz. each) chunk-style tuna
2 tablespoons chopped onion
1 can (16 oz.) tomatoes
1 can (6 oz.) tomato paste
1 teaspoon whole caraway seed
1 teaspoon salt
¼ teaspoon ground black pepper
2 eggs, slightly beaten
¼ cup crumbled Bleu cheese
¾ cup fine dry bread crumbs
¼ teaspoon whole marjoram leaves, crumbled
2 tablespoons oil or butter or margarine
3 quarts boiling water
1 tablespoon salt
8 oz. spaghetti
Grated Parmesan cheese

Drain tuna, reserving any oil. Place together 2 tablespoons tuna oil and onion in small saucepan over low heat. Cook until onion is golden, stirring often. Add tomatoes, tomato paste, caraway seed, salt, and pepper, stirring until blended. Cover and simmer 20 minutes over low heat, stirring occasionally. Mix together tuna, eggs, cheese, ½ cup bread crumbs, and marjoram until blended. Shape tuna mixture into small patties. Coat patties with remaining crumbs. Heat oil in large skillet or frying pan over medium heat until hot but not smoking; add tuna patties; cook 4 to 5 minutes or until lightly browned, turning frequently. Add patties to tomato sauce; simmer covered 5 minutes. Meanwhile, boil water with salt in saucepan over high heat; gradually add spaghetti so that water continues boiling. Cook uncovered, stirring occasionally until tender; drain in colander. Serve spaghetti with sauce and tuna patties spooned on top. Sprinkle with Parmesan cheese. Makes 6 servings.

NOTE: This makes a welcome change from the usual spaghetti and meat balls.

PLANKED SHAD

1 (5-lbs.) shad, dressed and boned
Salt
Ground black pepper
3 to 4 tablespoons melted butter or margarine
3 cups riced or mashed potatoes
3 egg yolks
½ to ¾ teaspoon salt
⅛ teaspoon ground black pepper
2 to 4 tablespoons melted butter or margarine
¾ cup hot cooked, seasoned, diced carrots
¾ cup hot cooked, seasoned green beans
¾ cup hot cooked, seasoned peas
¾ cup hot cooked, seasoned, diced beets
6 to 8 broiled mushroom caps
2 small tomatoes, cut in half and broiled
Crisp watercress sprigs
Lemon wedges

Heat oak or hickory plank in hot (425°F.) oven 10 minutes. Spread boned fish out flat; lightly salt and pepper both sides; brush with melted butter. Oil the heated wooden plank; place shad, skin side down, in center. Bake in preheated hot oven (425°F.) 15 to 18 minutes or until nearly done. Meanwhile mix potatoes together with egg yolks, salt, and pepper; beat until light; fill into cake decorating bag having large star tube attachment; dress heavy border of potatoes through star tube around fish inside edge of plank; dress potato sections from fish to border with spaces large enough to hold vegetables. Brush fish and potatoes with melted butter. Return to oven. Bake 6 to 8 minutes or until fish is done and potatoes are golden. Fill potato sections around fish with vegetables, arranging them colorfully. Garnish with watercress and lemon. Place plank on large, napkin-covered platter; serve from plank. Makes 6 to 8 servings.

NOTE: This method can also be used for whole bluefish, bass, or whitefish. Any or all of the cooked vegetables specified in list of ingredients can be used.

☙ SAN FRANCISCO (EARLY DAYS) OYSTER LOAF

1 (1 lb.) loaf unsliced white bread
1 to 1½ cups butter or margarine, melted
1 quart shucked raw oysters
2 eggs, beaten
¼ cup milk
½ teaspoon celery salt
½ teaspoon onion salt
¼ teaspoon ground white pepper
Fine cracker crumbs
Fat or oil for shallow-frying
½ lb. bacon, cooked crisp
Crisp parsley sprigs
2 lemons, cut into 8 wedges

Trim crusts from top and sides of bread. Slice off loaf top 1-inch thick; set aside. Hollow out remaining loaf, leaving ⅜-inch-thick side walls and base, thus making a bread-box. Save leftover crumbs to use later in casseroles or other dishes. Generously brush cut-off top slice and inside and outside of bread loaf box with butter. Place both in baking pan; bake in pre-heated moderate oven (375°F.) 12 to 15 minutes or until pale golden; remove from oven. Drain oysters. Mix together eggs, milk, celery salt, onion salt, and pepper; pour into shallow bowl. Dip oysters into cracker crumbs, then into egg mixture, and back into cracker crumbs until evenly crumb-coated. Fry oysters, without crowding, in 2-inch deep hot fat about 2 minutes or until delicately browned; remove and drain on absorbent paper.

Place half of bacon in prepared bread box on heat-proof serving platter; fill with oysters; top with remaining bacon; cover with top slice; surround loaf with any remaining oysters. Bake in a moderate oven (375°F.) 5 to 6 minutes or until piping hot. Garnish with parsley and lemon wedges and serve. Makes 6 servings.

◆§ PORGIES BAKED IN ALUMINUM FOIL

6 large porgies, dressed
Salt
Ground black pepper
Aluminum foil
3 tablespoons melted butter or margarine
2 medium tomatoes, thickly sliced
3 tablespoons chopped parsley
Salt and ground black pepper

Wash and wipe porgies dry. Sprinkle inside and outside with salt and pepper. Place each porgie on square aluminum foil large enough to wrap the fish. Brush fish on all sides with melted butter. Place one tomato slice on each fish; sprinkle with parsley. Salt and pepper the tomato. Wrap foil around fish, making a drug-store fold on top and folding the sides upward. Bake in pan in pre-heated hot oven (450°F.) 25 to 30 minutes or until done. Fish is done when flesh flakes easily under the gentle prodding of a fork. Serve fish in foil. Use same method for any small fish. Makes 6 servings.

◆§ GOLDEN PANNED BUTTERFISH

6 butterfish, dressed
Salt and ground black pepper
½ cup white or yellow corn meal
¼ cup flour
½ cup milk
¼ cup butter or margarine
Lemon wedges
Crisp watercress
2 tablespoons French dressing

Wash fish. Drain and pat dry; season generously inside and out with salt and pepper. Mix together corn meal and flour; place on square of waxed paper or foil. Dip fish into milk to moisten; roll in corn meal mixture to coat evenly. Heat butter in large skillet or frying pan over moderate heat until frothy; add fish, side by side, without crowding. Cook 5 to 6 minutes or until browned on under side; turn and cook 3 to 4 minutes or until browned on other side. Serve on heated platter garnished with lemon and watercress; sprinkle French dressing on cress just before serving. Makes 6 servings.

POACHED SALMON

- 1½ quarts water
- ¼ cup white vinegar
- 1 tablespoon salt
- ¼ teaspoon ground black pepper
- ¼ teaspoon whole allspice
- 1 sprig fresh or teaspoon whole dill seed
- 1 bay leaf
- 1 sprig celery leaves
- 1 medium onion, quartered
- 1 carrot, sliced
- 2 lbs. salmon, in one piece
- Hollandaise, or mayonnaise, or lemon sauce

Place water, vinegar, salt, pepper, allspice, dill, bay leaf, celery, onion and carrot in kettle over moderate heat; simmer covered one hour. Strain broth, discarding spices and vegetables. Return broth to kettle; place over low heat. Place fish on heat-proof plate; place plate on square of cheese cloth large enough to cover the fish. Gather cheese cloth together at the top; tie to enclose fish. Lower fish into liquid in kettle. Simmer covered 20 to 25 minutes or until done, keeping the water steaming but not bubbling, as in poaching. Lift out fish by grasping cheese cloth at the top; drain, reserving 1 cup broth for lemon sauce for fish, and unwrap. Serve hot with Hollandaise or lemon sauce or cold with mayonnaise or lemon sauce. Makes 4 servings.

Lemon Sauce for Fish

2 tablespoons butter or margarine
2 tablespoons flour
½ cup light cream or milk
1 cup fish broth
¼ cup fresh lemon juice
1 egg yolk
½ teaspoon salt
2 tablespoons chopped parsley

Heat butter in small saucepan over moderate heat until frothy; add flour, stirring until frothy. Gradually add cream, then broth, stirring constantly. Mix together lemon juice and egg yolk; add to hot mixture, stirring constantly. Cook until slightly thickened and smooth, stirring constantly. Add salt; remove from heat; add parsley. Serve hot or cold with salmon or any fish. Makes 1½ cups sauce.

5. Poultry

TO BONE CUT-UP CHICKEN PARTS FOR FRYING

Separate legs from thighs of chicken by cutting at joints. Split breast in half. Cut off wings.

To bone legs use a sharp knife, and cut deep into bone and all around, just under the big joint where it joins the thigh. Scrape along leg bone, pushing meat down all around the bone. Grasp the bone in one hand and pull leg meat down with the other and cut away. Turn boneless leg inside out as finger of a glove and so return the skin to the surface.

For thighs, cut a slit on inside flesh just to and along round bone; then lift and pry out bone. Ease flesh away from flat hip bone. Pry out flat thigh bone by scraping with knife tip. Pull flesh free while aiding with knife-tip scraping and prying close to bones.

Ease breast bone away from flesh by inserting knife blade close to the bone. Cut away rib bones using knife blade in flat position. Leave wings whole.

This takes a little practice and determination, but is

worth the trouble, especially where there are small children who might get in trouble over some of the bones.

Save bones to make a little chicken broth.

Fry chicken in any way desired.

◈§ FRIED CHICKEN

- 1 (2½ to 3 lbs.) ready-to-cook broiler-fryer, quartered
- ½ cup flour
- 1 teaspoon salt
- ¼ teaspoon ground black pepper
- 1½ cups fat or oil for shallow frying
- 2 tablespoons flour
- ½ cup water
- 1 cup milk
- Salt and ground black pepper to taste

Remove chicken bones if desired. Coat with mixture of flour, salt, and pepper. Heat fat in large skillet or frying pan until hot but not smoking. Add chicken, skin-side down. Cover and cook over high heat 8 to 10 minutes or until golden on underside. Turn pieces over. Cover and cook over very low heat 12 to 14 minutes or until done. Lift out chicken onto heated serving platter. Pour out any excess fat. Sprinkle flour into pan. Add water and milk; stir well. Cook over low heat until gravy forms. Season to taste. Serve gravy with chicken. Do not strain. Makes 4 servings.

◈§ LEMONADE FRIED CHICKEN

You should have seen this cooked chicken devoured after the show went off the air! It certainly made a big hit. I believe this is the easiest recipe to come my way within the last decade. Of course, that small can of frozen lemonade concentrate represents much squeezing of lemons. Having that lemonade all ready except for the adding of water is just like having an extra pair of hands to do that job for you. This is just an example of the help available in the supermarkets today. Since you know you can buy the chicken already cut up, you can see that this represents little work. The results make it look fantasically complicated to prepare. No one would believe that you hadn't slaved for 2 or 3 hours to put this dish together. There was no question about it in the whole studio or in the minds of our viewers that this recipe rated the gold skillet award. I've served it with a green vegetable, such as peas or broccoli, and a baked potato. If you're having your mother-in-law to dinner for the first time, and want to impress her that you are an excellent cook, why don't you prepare the lemonade fried chicken for her?

1 can (6 oz.) frozen concentrated lemonade
¾ cup water
1 (2 to 2½ lbs.) ready-to-cook broiler-fryer, cut up
⅓ cup flour
1 teaspoon salt
¼ teaspoon ground black pepper
½ cup oil
2 tablespoons melted butter or margarine

Mix together lemonade and water; pour over chicken in bowl. Refrigerate 2 hours or longer. Drain chicken and retain liquid. Mix together flour, salt, and pepper in small paper bag or on waxed paper. Add well-drained chicken. Grasp bag closed and shake to flour the chicken evenly. Heat oil in large skillet or frying pan over moderate heat. Add floured chicken; cook until evenly browned, turning the pieces over carefully. Remove chicken and arrange in single layer in shallow baking pan. Brush chicken with melted butter. Add reserved lemonade. Bake uncovered in a moderate oven (350°F.) about 50 minutes to 1 hour, or until chicken is tender. Spoon lemonade in pan over chicken several times as it bakes. Makes 4 to 5 servings.

CHICKEN BREAST WITH PINEAPPLE, CARROTS, AND GREEN PEPPERS

2 broiler-fryer chicken breasts, split
2 tablespoons oil
1 teaspoon bottled sauce for gravy
1 teaspoon salt
½ teaspoon onion salt
½ teaspoon celery salt
1 teaspoon ground ginger
1 cup pineapple juice, from canned pineapple chunks
2 cups diagonally sliced raw carrots
1 cup canned pineapple chunks, drained
2 small green peppers, cut into 1-inch strips
1 teaspoon cornstarch
1 tablespoon cold water
Hot cooked rice

Using a sharp knife, cut chicken meat from bones, leaving breasts intact. Discard skin and cut meat into 1½-inch cubes. Place oil in large skillet or frying pan over moderate heat. Add chicken and bottled sauce. Cook until evenly browned, stirring constantly. Add seasonings, pineapple juice, and sliced carrots; cover and simmer about 25 to 30 minutes or until chicken and carrots are tender. Add pineapple chunks and green peppers. Cover and simmer about 5 minutes. Mix together cornstarch and water, until smooth. Gradually add to simmering chicken while stirring constantly until the broth around chicken is thickened and clear. Cook 3 to 4 minutes. Serve with hot cooked rice. Makes 6 servings.

CHICKEN AND ROSEMARY

4 tablespoons olive oil
1 (3 to 3½ lbs.) ready-to-cook broiler-fryer, cut up
1 clove garlic, minced
2 teaspoons whole, crumbled rosemary leaves
¼ cup wine vinegar
¼ cup water
½ cup sherry
1 teaspoon salt
⅛ teaspoon ground black pepper

Heat oil in large skillet or frying pan. Add chicken. Cook, turning frequently, about 15 minutes over moderate heat until browned on all sides. Lower heat. Add garlic, rosemary, vinegar, water, sherry, salt, and pepper. Cover and simmer 1¼ hours. Remove cover, turn up heat, and cook 10 to 12 minutes, or until well-glazed, turning once. Serve with Kasha (see page 41) and hot buttered peas. Makes 4 servings.

BONELESS CHICKEN BREASTS WITH HAM, SCALLIONS, AND MUSHROOMS

2 broiler-fryer chicken breasts, split
Salt and ground black pepper
1 slice boiled ham, quartered
2 scallions
4 (2½- to 3-inch) carrot strips
2 eggs, beaten
1 tablespoon flour
1 tablespoon cornstarch
½ teaspoon salt
Oil for frying
1 cup chicken broth from bones
Liquid drained from mushrooms
2 teaspoons cornstarch
1 tablespoon cold water
2 teaspoons soy sauce
1 can (4 oz.) whole mushrooms, drained

Remove bones from chicken breasts. Season chicken with salt and pepper. Boil bones in salted water to cover, for broth. Spread breasts skin-side down. Lay 1 piece boiled ham, ½ scallion, and 1 strip carrot across wide end of each chicken breast. Roll up and fasten with small skewers or tie with twine. Mix together eggs, flour, cornstarch, and salt, beating until smooth. Pour oil ½ inch deep into large skillet or frying pan. Heat until hot but not smoking (360°F.). Dip rolled chicken breasts in egg-flour-cornstarch mixture and let drip. Fry in heated oil, turning 2 or 3 times until evenly browned. Place browned chicken in shallow casserole. Bake in moderate oven (350°F.) 35 to 40 minutes or until done. Combine chicken broth from bones and mushroom liquid in small saucepan over moderate heat and bring to a boil. Mix together cornstarch, water, and soy sauce, stirring until smooth; add to broth stirring constantly, and cook about 2 to 3 minutes or until slightly thickened and clear. Add mushrooms, reheat, and pour over chicken. Makes 4 servings.

NOTE: Serve with cooked rice or buttered or fried noodles.

CHICKEN, HAM, AND NOODLE STEW

Bring on the gang—this is their dish! You'll notice we've presented many dishes for a gang because we realize that Americans are pretty sociable eaters and any one of these recipes can be cut down to family size and served any day in the week just to the family. Imagine, by being able to throw things into a pot and letting them cook, you can make a dish that you'd dare give to a very fastidious group of guests. That's what this chicken, ham, and noodle stew is—it's superb! Has such a nice aroma as it cooks too. This dish goes back to my college days because that's where I first learned about it. I have used it over and over again. Every time I make it, it meets with new success. Americans love chicken and they seem to love noodles—and they love ham. Here are the three favorites all cooked together in one pot. I have a few standbys that I lean on for serving a group and this is certainly one of them. Maybe it'll get to be one of yours, too.

2 (4½ to 5 lbs. each) ready-to-cook stewing chickens, cut up
2 slices (1-inch thick) smoked (cook-before-eating) ham
5 to 6 stalks celery, diced
2 carrots, diced
2 to 3 bay leaves
3 quarts hot water
1½ tablespoons salt
1 teaspoon ground black pepper
2½ lbs. green or yellow egg noodles

Place chicken with giblets, neck, and any fat in large kettle. (See *) Dice ham into 1-inch cubes and add with any bone, fat, or skin. Add celery, carrots, bay leaves, hot water, salt, and pepper. Cover and simmer about 3½ to 3¾ hours, or until tender, but not quite fork-tender. Add noodles, pushing them down into broth around chicken. Cover and simmer 25 to 30 minutes or until noodles are tender and have completely absorbed the broth. Serve for parties, with tossed green salad, or cooked green bean and celery salad and garlic bread. Makes about 20 servings, if there are no seconds. (* May be cooked in 2 Dutch ovens.)

☙ HAM-CRAB STUFFED CHICKEN DRUMSTICKS

8 raw chicken drumsticks
½ cup ground cooked ham
1 can (6½ oz.) crab meat, flaked
2 tablespoons cornstarch
1 egg, slightly beaten
2 tablespoons water
¼ cup oil
2 tablespoons chopped onion
½ cup canned mushrooms, undrained
½ cup bouillon or water
2 teaspoons soy sauce
Salt, to taste
1 teaspoon lemon juice
Hot cooked rice
4 broiled tomato halves for garnish

Remove bones from each drumstick by cutting through flesh to bone all around upper joint. Grasp bone and force meat down along bone with knife. Cut off bone. Invert the cut off leg meat so the skin is on the outside. Combine ham and crab meat; mix lightly. Fill hollows in chicken with ham-crab mixture; close openings at the top with toothpicks. Coat with cornstarch; moisten with blended egg and water mixture. Heat oil in large skillet or frying pan over moderate heat. Add chicken and brown evenly, turning occasionally. Add onion, mushrooms, bouillon, soy sauce, salt, and lemon juice. Cover and simmer about 1 hour or until tender. Serve with hot cooked rice and garnish with broiled tomatoes. Makes 4 servings.

☙ CHICKEN CHILI

1 (2½ to 3 lbs.) ready-to-cook broiler-fryer chicken, cut up
2 cups boiling water
½ cup butter or margarine
2 onions, chopped
2 cups canned tomatoes
1 tablespoon chili powder
2 tablespoons wine vinegar
1 tablespoon brown sugar
2 teaspoons salt
2 cloves garlic
2 to 3 slices toasted Italian or French bread
Hot cooked rice or macaroni

Using sharp knife, cut all chicken meat off bones (see page 79). Dice meat small and reserve. Combine bones and boiling water in saucepan. Cover and simmer about 1 hour to make broth. Heat butter in large skillet or frying pan; add chicken; cook and stir 20 to 25 minutes or until browned. Add onions and cook until lightly browned, stirring constantly. Place browned chicken and onions in medium saucepan. Add tomatoes, strained broth from chicken bones, chili powder, vinegar, brown sugar, and salt; blend. Cover and simmer about 1½ hours or until chicken is tender and flavors have blended. Rub garlic into both sides of toasted bread. Break bread into small pieces and add to simmering chili. Cover and cook about 15 minutes more or until bread is completely dissolved and slightly thickens the juices. Serve over hot cooked rice or macaroni. Makes 6 servings.

☙ OVEN CHICKEN CROQUETTES

- 2½ cups chopped cooked chicken
- 1 cup finely chopped celery
- 1 cup soft bread crumbs
- 2 tablespoons mayonnaise or salad dressing
- 1 egg, slightly beaten
- 1 teaspoon salt
- ¼ teaspoon ground black pepper
- ¼ cup melted butter or margarine
- ½ cup dry bread crumbs

Combine all ingredients except melted butter and dry bread crumbs. Mix thoroughly and chill about 1 hour. Shape into 6 croquettes or patties. Roll each in melted butter, then in bread crumbs. Place in shallow baking pan. Bake in a moderate oven (375°F.) about 40 to 45 minutes, or until golden brown, turning once during the baking period. Serve plain, or with mushroom or celery sauce. Makes 6 servings.

☙ BRAISED CHICKEN GIZZARDS WITH MUSHROOMS

- 1 lb. cleaned chicken gizzards
- ½ cup flour
- 4 tablespoons butter or margarine
- 2 teaspoons bottled sauce for gravy
- 2 teaspoons salt
- ½ onion, chopped
- 2 cups boiling water
- 2 tablespoons butter or margarine
- ½ lb. fresh mushrooms, sliced
- 3 cups hot cooked rice or Chinese fried noodles

Trim gizzards removing all fat. Wash and drain thoroughly; cut across into ¾-inch slices. Pat very dry; coat thoroughly with flour. Heat butter in large skillet or frying pan; add gizzards; cook about 8 to 10 minutes, or until browned, stirring frequently. Add bottled sauce, salt, and onion; cook about 4 minutes longer, or until onions are soft, stirring constantly. Add water; simmer, tightly covered, about 2 to 3 hours (20 minutes in pressure cooker), or until gizzards are tender, replenishing water, if needed. Meanwhile, heat butter in large skillet or frying pan; add mushrooms. Cook about 8 to 10 minutes, or until mushrooms are lightly browned, stirring frequently. Add to gizzards. Stir well; cover and simmer about 8 to 10 minutes, or until flavors have blended. Serve on platter in center of rice or fried noodle ring. Makes 6 servings.

POLENTA RING WITH CHICKEN LIVERS

1½ quarts water
1 tablespoon salt
2 cups yellow corn meal
2 cups water
3 slices lean bacon, diced
4 tablespoons butter or margarine
1 lb. chicken livers, diced
1 lb. fresh mushrooms, sliced
Salt and ground black pepper to taste
¼ teaspoon ground sage leaves
¼ cup dry white wine

Bring water and salt to a boil in medium saucepan. Mix together corn meal and cold water; slowly add to boiling water, stirring constantly. Cook over very low heat about 50 minutes, stirring often. Turn into greased 2-quart ring mold. Keep hot by placing mold in shallow pan of hot water. Meanwhile, cook bacon in skillet or frying pan until crisp. Add butter, chicken livers, and mushrooms. Cook about 15 to 20 minutes or until browned, stirring frequently. Add salt, pepper, sage, and wine; blend. Lower heat; cook uncovered about 3 minutes, stirring occasionally. Turn polenta ring onto platter. Pour chicken livers into center. Makes 6 to 8 servings.

CHICKEN WINGS WITH SPANISH RICE

- 2 lbs. chicken wings, from roasting or broiler-fryer chickens
- ¼ cup olive oil
- 1 cup chopped onions
- 1 clove garlic, crushed
- 1 cup raw regular rice
- 2 teaspoons salt
- ¼ teaspoon ground black pepper
- 1 cup canned tomatoes and liquid
- 1¼ cups bouillon
- ¼ teaspoon ground saffron
- 1 cup cooked peas
- 2 pimientos, diced

Pick chicken wings free of pin feathers; wash, drain, and pat dry. Heat oil over moderate heat in large skillet or frying pan until hot but not smoking; add onions and garlic; cook until soft and lightly browned, stirring constantly; remove onions and garlic from skillet and set aside. Add chicken wings to oil in pan; cook uncovered until evenly browned, turning frequently. Place chicken wings and onions into saucepan. Add rice, salt, pepper, tomatoes, and bouillon. Dissolve saffron in 1 tablespoon hot water; add to chicken. Cover and simmer 45 to 50 minutes or until rice and chicken are tender and rice has absorbed all the liquid. Add peas and pimientos, gently folding together. Reheat and serve. Makes 4 to 6 servings.

BORDEAUX BARBECUED DUCKLING

(Dedicated to Tex Antoine)

- ½ cup orange marmalade
- 1 tablespoon soy sauce
- 1 teaspoon salt
- 1 (3½ to 4 lbs.) ready-to-cook duckling, quartered
- 1 tablespoon butter or margarine
- 1 tablespoon flour
- ¾ cup dry white Bordeaux wine
- 1 tablespoon wine vinegar
- ¼ cup consomme
- ¼ teaspoon ground black pepper

Mix together marmalade, soy sauce, and salt; place half the mixture aside. Grill duckling over glowing coals 45 minutes or until crispy and done, turning and basting frequently with half of marmalade mixture. Meanwhile, heat butter in small saucepan over moderate heat until frothy. Add flour, stirring 1 to 2 minutes, or until lightly browned. Add wine, vinegar, consomme, and pepper; blend. Cover and simmer 8 to 10 minutes. Add remaining marmalade mixture; simmer covered for 5 minutes. Serve duckling on heated platter with marmalade sauce spooned on top. Makes 4 servings.

☙ CHINESE PLUM DUCK

Cooking with peanut oil is typical of many Chinese dishes; it imparts a delicate, illusive flavor without appreciable richness. When the first step is browning the food in peanut oil, care must be taken not to let the oil smoke; this simple precaution assures a delectable flavor in the finished dish.

1 (4 lbs.) ready-to-cook duckling, cut into pieces
⅓ cup soy sauce
½ cup peanut oil
½ cup mashed, skinned, and pitted canned purple plums
½ cup syrup drained from plums
Small piece preserved ginger, cut into slivers
½ cup chopped scallion tops
1 clove garlic, minced
2 tablespoons bottled sweet duck sauce
2 tablespoons cornstarch
¼ cup cold water
Hot cooked rice
Bottled sweet duck sauce for dunking

Coat duck pieces generously with soy sauce. Place oil in large skillet or frying pan over moderate heat until hot but not smoking; add duck; cook 8 to 10 minutes or until golden brown, turning pieces frequently. Pour off excess fat; lower heat. Mix remaining soy sauce together with plums, plum syrup, ginger, scallions, garlic, and duck sauce; pour over duck. Simmer, tightly covered, 30 to 40 minutes or until tender. Lift duck onto heated serving platter. Mix together cornstarch and water; add to pan juices, stirring constantly. Cook 3 to 4 minutes or until thickened and smooth, stirring frequently. Pour over duck. Serve with hot rice. Serve individual portions of bottled duck sauce for dunking fork-sized pieces of the duck. Makes 4 to 6 servings.

NOTE: Good accompaniments are Chinese tea, with dessert of preserved kumquats and Chinese almond cookies.

DUCKLING IN ASPIC

1 (5-6 lbs.) ready-to-cook duckling
3 cups water
2 teaspoons salt
2 to 3 celery tops
1 medium onion, sliced
6 to 8 whole cloves
¼ teaspoon peppercorns
2 tablespoons plain, unflavored gelatine
½ cup cold water
¼ cup vinegar
½ teaspoon garlic salt
½ cup claret
12 stuffed olives, sliced
6 green pepper strips (¼-inch)
6 pimiento strips
1 cup diced celery

Cut duckling into quarters. Place in kettle with giblets and neck. Add water, salt, celery tops, onion, cloves, and peppercorns. Bring to a boil. Cover and simmer 45 to 50 minutes or until fork-tender, over low heat. Cool 45 minutes in broth. Lift out duck; strain broth and set aside to cool. Remove skin and bones from duck meat; dice meat into small cubes. Soften gelatine in cold water. Skim fat off duck broth. Measure 1½ cups broth into small saucepan; bring to a boil; remove from heat. Add gelatine, stirring until dissolved. Add vinegar, garlic salt, and claret, mixing until blended; pour enough into an 8½ x 4½ x 2½-inch loaf pan to barely cover the bottom. Arrange sliced olives, green pepper, and pimiento strips in a pattern in the gelatine; chill until firmed. Cool gelatine broth until it begins to thicken; add duck meat and celery, mixing until blended; pour into loaf pan over firmed bottom layer. Cover with waxed paper or aluminum foil. Chill several hours or overnight or until firm enough to slice. Unmold and serve sliced with Waldorf salad. Makes 8 to 10 servings.

SKINNED DUCK WITH APRICOTS

- 1 (5 to 6 lbs.) ready-to-cook duckling
- 2 teaspoons bottled sauce for gravy
- 1 clove garlic, minced
- Salt
- 2 tablespoons butter or margarine
- 1 cup canned apricot nectar
- 2 tablespoons cornstarch
- ¼ cup cold water
- ½ cup dried apricots, soaked about 1 hour in warm water to cover

Cut through skin along center of duck breast from neck to vent, with sharp, pointed knife. Grasping skin with one hand, loosen by running knife underneath the fatty skin layer close to flesh, at the same time peeling back layer of skin and fat. Skin and quarter duck. Place in bowl. Brush with bottled sauce, garlic, and salt. Melt butter in large skillet or chicken fryer over moderate heat. Add duck; cook until pieces are browned evenly, turning pieces 2 or 3 times. Add apricot nectar. Bring to a boil; cover tightly and simmer about 45 minutes or until tender. Mix together cornstarch and water; add to broth, stirring constantly until juice is slightly thickened. Drain and add apricots. Cover and simmer over low heat about 10 minutes. Makes 4 servings.

ROTISSERIE-ROASTED SMALL BROAD-BREAST TURKEY

This basting trick will be the talk of your neighborhood . . . just wait. This is a he-man's job and should be reserved for the man of the house: I suggest you plan an audience for this bird as it roasts. What an idea for a party!

- 1 (8 lbs.) ready-to-cook broad-breast turkey
- 1 teaspoon ground ginger
- 1 teaspoon chili powder
- 1 teaspoon ground sage leaves
- 2 teaspoons salt
- ¼ teaspoon ground black pepper
- Salad or olive oil
- 2 stalks celery with leaves attached
- ½ cup sherry

Wash turkey, thoroughly rinsing the inside; pat outside and inside dry. Mix together ginger, chili powder, sage, salt, and pepper; rub mixture into crop and body cavity. Close body opening with skewers and lace with twine; pull neck skin to back; fasten skin to back with skewer. Fold wing tips under and lock under first wing joint. Tie legs together with twine and wind twine around tail. Place turkey on spit, balancing in true center position. Brush entire outside with oil. Pre-heat roaster for 10 minutes at high heat. Reduce heat to medium. Place spitted turkey in roaster. Roast about 1½ to 2 hours or until done, basting every 15 or 20 minutes as follows: grasp celery stalk ends; dip leaves into sherry; pass the wine-dripping leaves over the bird; repeat dipping and basting, using more sherry if needed. Makes 10 to 12 servings.

YOUNG TURKEY CACCIATORE

¼ cup flour
1½ teaspoons salt
½ (5½ to 6 lbs.) ready-to-cook young frying turkey, cut into small pieces
½ cup olive or salad oil
1 small onion, sliced
1 green pepper, diced
1 clove garlic, minced
1 cup sliced fresh or canned mushrooms
1 can (6 oz.) thick tomato paste
1 cup bouillon, or bouillon and liquid from canned mushrooms
1 teaspoon salt
1 teaspoon sugar
⅛ teaspoon ground black pepper
2 pimientos, diced

Mix together flour and salt; coat turkey pieces with mixture. Heat oil in large skillet or frying pan over moderate heat until hot but not smoking. Add turkey; cook uncovered 15 to 20 minutes or until evenly browned, turning pieces often. Add onion, green pepper, garlic, mushrooms, tomato paste, bouillon, salt, sugar, and pepper. Cover and simmer 1½ to 1¾ hours or until tender. Add pimiento and cook 5 minutes longer. Makes 6 servings.

FLAMING ROAST ROCK CORNISH GAME HENS

3 tablespoons butter or margarine
1 onion, minced
½ cup chopped cooked ham
½ cup chopped fresh or canned mushrooms
1½ cups cooked wild rice (½ cup raw rice steamed tender in 1½ cups water and 1 teaspoon salt, covered over low heat about 30 to 45 minutes)
½ teaspoon salt
¼ teaspoon ground black pepper
¼ teaspoon ground thyme leaves
½ teaspoon ground marjoram leaves
¼ cup brandy
6 (1 lb each) ready-to-cook Rock Cornish Game Hens
Salt and ground pepper

3 to 4 tablespoons salad oil
1 teaspoon paprika
¼ cup sherry
¼ cup hot water
¼ cup brandy

Heat butter in skillet or frying pan; add onions; cook over moderate heat until golden brown, about 5 minutes, stirring constantly. Add ham, mushrooms, wild rice, salt, remaining seasonings, and brandy; mix well and set aside. Salt and pepper insides of hens. Pack ¾ full with wild rice stuffing and tie legs together. Fold wings back and under. Place stuffed birds in greased shallow casserole. Combine oil and paprika; let stand until paprika settles on the bottom. Pour carefully reddish oil off the top. Brush oil over birds. Roast uncovered in moderate oven (375°F.) about 1 to 1½ hours or until tender and nicely browned. Remove roasted birds to serving platter. Add sherry and hot water to juices in pan and cook 2 to 3 minutes, stirring brown bits from pan into gravy. Strain gravy over birds. Heat brandy, hold over birds at the table, and, in full view of diners, hold lighted match to brandy. When it flames, pour over birds and let burn until flame dies out. Makes 6 servings.

6. *Meat*

ROASTING

Expertness in cooking meats comes with practice and self-confidence. The best Sunday or company dinner is still a "Roast." Roasting is easy on the cook. A roast needs no watching or basting; but it does need timing. Over-cooked rib roast of beef is ruined roast beef for the average American taste. Under-cooked roast pork should never be served. In France, roast lamb is served and relished rare. Americans prefer roast lamb medium to well-done. Everyone relishes a rich brown crisp-crusted roast turkey, chicken, duck, or goose.

Tender cuts of meat and young birds are used for roasting. Less tender cuts of meat are not suited to this method of cooking. They need a different treatment, such as braising, boiling, stewing, or steaming, to turn them into delicious main dishes. To roast means to cook in dry heat, uncovered. There is a relatively new technique for roasting meats, and that is to roast them wrapped in aluminum foil. This requires higher heat and shorter cooking time. Timetables and directions for this method are included on the descriptive labels of the aluminum foil packages.

To cook a succulent, brown, mouth-watering roast, check timetable, allowing enough time for meat to finish twenty minutes before meal time. This allows time for making the gravy and for the meat to set. It also makes carving easier.

Always pre-heat oven to required temperature.

Do not wash meat. Sanitarily packaged meat cuts of today don't even need wiping. If necessary, wipe with paper towels.

Season meat. Salt barely penetrates into meat surface, and not enough to draw out the juices. Seasoning ahead eliminates forgetting to do it when you get busy with the meal. I always season the raw roast.

When using a meat thermometer (and I recommend it as a "must" for inexperienced cooks), insert it carefully. Plunge a skewer into the thickest lean part of the meat and so make an opening for the thermometer stem. Insert thermometer with bulb resting in the lean center of the roast, away from fat, bones, and gristle.

Place meat, fat side up, on rack in open pan. Rib roasts do not need a rack. The bones form the rack.

Do not flour.

Do not add liquid unless recipe directs.

Follow timetable for roasting.

Do not baste unless recipe directs.

Do not watch. Set timer or alarm clock.

When meat thermometer registers "done," check reading carefully, in case it shifted position, by gently pushing the bulb deeper into the meat. If thermometer drops, roast a little longer until it registers correct temperature.

ABOUT THE GRAVY

Pan juices are the basis of fine gravy. Pour excess fat out of roasting pan. Dissolve all the juices in the pan with boiling water, scraping away the dried, roasted juices that cling to the pan. These are flavor-givers. Measure the liquid. Pour it into a saucepan. To serve "natural gravy," boil this until it is concentrated and some of the water evaporates. Strain. This is *au jus* gravy. To thicken it slightly, allow 1 tablespoon flour or ½ tablespoon cornstarch or potato starch for each cup of liquid. Moisten the flour or starch until runny and smooth. Stir into the boiling pan liquid. Boil until clear and smooth. Season to taste. Strain it if you like.

Or, you can measure 1 tablespoon pan fat for each cup of gravy you want. Heat the fat in a saucepan. Stir in an equal amount of flour. Place over heat. Stir in 1 cup of the hot pan liquid made with water as above. Season. Cook and stir until thickened and smooth. To make a medium-thick gravy, use these proportions for every cup of gravy:

2 tablespoons fat
2 tablespoons flour
1 cup pan liquid

Cook as above.

What makes lumps in gravy? This question comes in so often. This is how I explain it on television:

Any starchy ingredient will thicken gravy. Milled flour, potato flour, tapioca, arrowroot, rice flour, or any cereal meal will thicken a liquid when boiled in it. The starch granules in a raw grated potato will, when stirred into boiling liquid or broth, thicken it. Barley and rice and tapioca, when boiled long enough to disintegrate, will promptly thicken the liquid. Some vegetables rich in vegetable gums also thicken liquids. Okra will thicken a boiling liquid. Various peoples of the globe use many products we would never think to use—sea-weed, for example, for thickening soups, broths, and sauces.

About those lumps. Gravies with lumps in them are always irritating. Adding a spoonful of dry flour or cornstarch to a cupful of boiling liquid would give us a pebbly lumpy mass. However, mix that same flour with a little cold water or milk or melted fat or oil and add it gradually to boiling liquid and the result is a smooth evenly thickened mass—no lumps. The process can be reversed by blending starch or flour and the fat, and gradually adding the liquid. This is the secret to lumpless gravies. The starch granules in dry flour swell and stick to each other like glue the moment flour is put into boiling water. Mix cold water, milk, or oil with dry flour and each starch granule gets a coating of that material. When you add this mixture to boiling water, the starch granules swell but the coating of water or fat keeps them from sticking to each other. They float freely and you get a smoothly thickened sauce. When you sprinkle dry flour into boiling water, it falls in small lumps containing several million flour-starch cells. Only the outer layer of starch cells contact the boiling water. These swell and cling to each other like glue. They trap the dry flour inside, like a core. This makes a lump. Multiply this by hundreds of thousands in a gravy and you have a lumpy gravy.

OTHER WAYS TO COOK MEAT

Meats of less tender cuts can be *braised*. Braising means to first evenly brown the meat slowly, uncovered, in a small amount of fat. Seasoning and a small amount of liquid are added; then the meat is cooked, covered, over low heat until it is tender. The steam created inside the covered pot supplies the moist-heat needed to soften and braise less tender cuts. Since the steam alone does the cooking, the meat will have better flavor if it is placed on a rack and kept out of the liquid. Care must be taken not to overcook, as this makes the meat stringy. "Fork-tender" and firm enough to slice are the watch words for braising. Pot roasts and chicken fricassee are common dishes cooked by braising. Other terms for braising are "potting" and "smothering." Braising can be started on top of the stove and finished in the oven. The cover can be lifted off the pot at the end of the cooking time and the meat browned by the dry oven heat.

Boiling is cooking the covered meat in boiling water at 212°F. at sea level. The heat is controlled to keep the liquid bubbling gently. New England Boiled Dinner, tongues, and corned beef are cooked by boiling. Less tender fowl and less tender cuts of meat are boiled to give a rich broth as well as to cook the meat.

Simmering is cooking covered over low heat, under boiling temperature, and controlling the heat so no bubbles form. Stews are simmered.

Pan-broiling means to cook uncovered on a heated griddle or in a hot dry skillet or frying pan without fat. If fat oozes out of the meat, it should be poured out as cooking proceeds. Thin steaks and chops that would dry out in broiling are best pan-broiled. To pan-broil steaks or chops ½ to ¾-inch thick:

Heat skillet or griddle.
Rub lightly with fat or oiled soft paper.
Place meat on hot surface.

Do not cover.
Do not add water.
Brown on one side.
Turn and brown other side.
Reduce heat.

Cook 3 to 4 minutes on each side, turning to cook evenly until done to suit. Season. Top meat with melted butter or margarine. Frying pan may be rinsed out with a little hot water; this can be seasoned to taste and poured over the meat as gravy.

Broiling means to cook by direct heat, under broiler heat, over hot coals, or between two hot surfaces. To broil meats, follow manufacturer's directions for operating the broiler. Turn broiler regulator to broiling position. Pre-heat, following directions of manufacturer, generally 10 minutes. If there is no thermostat, turn to medium heat. Line broiler pan under rack with aluminum foil; this catches drippings and saves scouring.

Lightly grease rack with bit of trimmed off meat fat or oiled soft paper. Place meat on rack. Insert broiler pan with meat, having meat surface 2 inches below heat for ¾ to 1-inch-thick steak or chops, and 3 to 4 inches for thick meat cuts. Season when time to turn over; season topside when done.

Frying means to cook food immersed in hot fat or oil. Cooking in a small amount of fat is to pan-fry, or *saute*. Fried chicken is usually pan-fried.

Cooking in deep fat is called *deep-fat frying*. Use deep-fat fryer with removable wire basket. Use enough shortening or salad oil to completely cover the food, with enough unfilled space in kettle so fat won't bubble over during frying. Butter or margarine cannot be used for deep-fat frying.

Food to be fried should not be wet—this causes spattering and boiling over, and it is dangerous. Have fat at proper temperature. Fat that isn't hot enough disintegrates the coating on food and soaks into food to be fried.

Don't overheat fat. Burnt fat is not wholesome and doesn't cook the food through. Always reheat fat to required temperature when frying several batches.

Lacking a thermometer or automatic fryer, use a 1-inch square of white bread to test frying temperature. Drop the bread into hot fat and time it. If it browns in 60 seconds, it's hot enogh for croquettes, doughnuts, French fries, and whole small fish. If it browns in 40 seconds, it's hot enough for fritters, onion rings, oysters, and thin fish fillets.

Food to be fried should be at room temperature.

TIMETABLE FOR BROILING STEAKS

(Broil each side for half of total time)

Thickness	*Rare*	*Medium*
1 inch	8–10 minutes*	12–14 minutes
1½ inches	14–16 minutes	18–20 minutes
2 inches	30–35 minutes	40–50 minutes
(For Chuck, Blade, or Round Steak when using Meat Tenderizer)		
1 inch	10–12 minutes	12–14 minutes
1½ inches	15 minutes	20 minutes
2 inches	20–25 minutes	25–30 minutes

*Time is for chilled meat from the refrigerator. All times given are approximate, since the terms "rare," "medium," and "well done" are relative. Cook your steaks the way you like them, using these figures as guides.

BROILING TENDERLOIN (FILET MIGNON)

Thickness	*Rare*	*Medium*
1 inch	8 minutes*	12–16 minutes
1½ inches	12–16 minutes	16–20 minutes

TIMETABLE FOR BROILING MEAT PATTIES

(Broil each side for half of total time)

Thickness	*Rare*	*Medium*
½ inch	4–5 minutes*	8–10 minutes
1 inch	8–10 minutes	14–16 minutes

PAN-BROILING AND PAN-FRYING MEAT PATTIES

Thickness	*Rare*	*Medium*
½ inch	2 minutes	6 minutes
1 inch	4 minutes	8 minutes

*Time is for chilled meat from the refrigerator. All times given are approximate, since the terms "rare," "medium," and "well done" are relative. Cook your meat patties the way you like them, using these figures as guides.

TIMETABLE FOR BEEF ROASTS

	Oven Tempera-ture	*Degree of Doneness*	*Min-utes per lb.**	*Meat Ther-mometer*
Standing Rib Roast (5–6 pounds)	325°F.	Rare	18–22	140°F.
		Medium	23–28	160°F.
		Well done	27–33	170°F.
Standing Rib Roast (7–8 pounds)	325°F.	Rare	17–19	140°F.
		Medium	20–23	160°F.
		Well done	25–29	170°F.

TIMETABLE FOR BEEF ROASTS (cont.)

	Oven Temperature	*Degree of Doneness*	*Minutes per lb.**	*Meat Thermometer*
Rolled Rib Roast	325°F.	Rare	27–33	140°F.
		Medium	32–39	160°F.
		Well done	37–44	170°F.
Beef Tenderloin Roast	450°F.	Rare	12–15	140°F.
Sirloin Tip (about 4 pounds, top grades)	325°F.	Rare	20–24	140°F.
		Medium	30–34	160°F.
		Well done	44–48	170°F.

*Time is for chilled meat from the refrigerator. The amount of bone, thickness of cut, and many other factors affect roasting time. Roast your meat the way you like it, using these figures as guides.

TIMETABLE FOR VEAL

(Roasted at 325°F.)

Cut	*Approximate Weight (lbs.)*	*Approximate Time (hours)**	*Meat Thermometer*
Leg	3–8	2–4	180°F.
Loin	5–6	3⅓–4	180°F.
Shoulder	3–5	2–3	180°F.
Rump	4–8	2⅔–4	180°F.

*Time is for chilled meat from the refrigerator.

TIMETABLE FOR LAMB

(Roasted at 325°F.)

Cut	*Approximate Weight (lbs.)*	*Approximate Time (hours)**	*Meat Thermometer*
Leg (full)	8–9	4–4½	175°F. (med.)
		4½–5	180°F. (well)
Leg ("American")	5–6	2½–3	175°F. (med.)
		3–3½	180°F. (well)
Crown	5–6	3½–4½	180°F.
Shoulder	3–5	1¾–3	180°F.
Rolled Shoulder	3–4	2–2½	180°F.

*Time is for chilled meat from the refrigerator.

TIMETABLE FOR BROILING LAMB STEAKS, CHOPS, PATTIES

(Broil each side for half of total time)

Cut	*Approximate Thickness (inches)*	*Approximate Time (minutes)**
Rib or Loin Chops	1	12–14
	1½	18–20
Double Chops	2	22–30
Shoulder Chops	1	16–18
Leg Steaks	1	16–18
Patties	1	20–22
Mutton Chops	1	20–22

*Time is for chilled meat from the refrigerator.

TIMETABLE FOR FRESH PORK

(Roasted at 325°F.)

Cut	*Approximate Weight (lbs.)*	*Approximate Time (hours)**	*Meat Thermometer*
Loin	2–3	1½–2	185°F.
Loin	5–7	3–4	185°F.
Shoulder (fresh picnic or Boston butt)	4–6	3–4	185°F.
Ham	6–8	4½–5½	185°F.
Crown Roast	4–6	3–4	185°F.

*Time is for chilled meat from the refrigerator. If pork is boned and rolled, add 10 minutes per pound.

TIMETABLE FOR HAMS

(Baked at 325°F.)

	Approximate Weight (lbs.)	*Approximate Time (hours)**	*Meat Thermometer*
Whole, Uncooked (cook-before-eating)	10–15	3–5	160°F.
Half, Uncooked (cook-before-eating)	5–7	2¼–3	160°F.
	8–10	3½–4	160°F.

TIMETABLE FOR HAMS (cont.)

	Approximate Weight (lbs.)	*Approximate Time (hours)**	*Meat Thermometer*
Whole, Cooked (ready-to-eat)	10–12	2–2½	140°F.
	12–15	2½–3	140°F.
	15–18	3–3½	140°F.
Half, Cooked (ready-to-eat)	5–8	1½	140°F.
	8–10	2	140°F.
PICNIC			
Uncooked (cook-before-eating)	4–7	2½–3¾	170°F.
	8–10	4–5	170°F.
Cooked (ready-to-eat)	4–6	1¼	130°F.
	7–10	1¾	130°F.
SHOULDER BUTT			
Uncooked (cook-before-eating)	2–4	1½–2⅓	170°F.

*Time is for chilled meat from the refrigerator.

ROAST FRESH HAM

There's no question these days about whether the fresh ham comes from a young porker. Streamlined, bred to definite dimensions of leg, hip, and waist, height and body length, thickness of fat layer under his skin, the porker of today rolls off the processing line with thousands of others like him. Hog on the hoof is now raised by the clock, protected against former pig afflictions, and rushed to market at the age when the meat is just right as to tenderness and flavor, and even to specific size of hams, chops, and bacon.

SPICY ROAST FRESH HAM

(Requires 2 days waiting period in refrigerator before roasting)

- 6 to 8 lb. fresh ham (fresh pork leg)
- 2 cups cider vinegar
- 2 cups bottled or canned apple juice
- 1 quart water
- ½ cup gin (optional)
- 1 teaspoon peppercorns
- 3 to 4 bay leaves
- ½ teaspoon whole cloves
- 2 cloves garlic, crushed
- 1 teaspoon ground sage leaves
- 1 tablespoon salt
- 3 tablespoons sugar
- 3 cups boiling water
- 3 tablespoons cornstarch
- ¼ cup cold water
- Salt and ground black pepper to taste

Wipe pork with damp cloth. Place in deep bowl or crock. Mix together vinegar, apple juice, water, gin, peppercorns, bay leaves, cloves, garlic, sage, and salt in saucepan; bring to a boil. Cool. Pour over meat in bowl. Refrigerate, covered, for about 2 days, turning meat 2 to 3 times each day. To roast, drain pork; strain liquid and reserve. Place pork, skin-side up, on rack in open pan. Pour 2 cups reserved liquid into pan. Roast in slow oven (325°F.) about 4½ to

5½ hours or until no trace of pink remains around center bone and meat is well done, basting often. Allow 45 minutes per pound roasting time. Remove ham from oven. Trim off rind; score fat, making diagonal cuts through fat to the meat. Sprinkle with sugar. Return to oven for about 20 minutes or until slightly glazed. Lift ham onto heated serving platter. For sauce, pour excess fat out of roasting pan. Add boiling water; stir in cornstarch mixed with cold water. Boil until clear and smooth. Season to taste. Pass with meat. Makes 12 to 14 servings.

GLAZED HAM

Scarcely a day goes by that I don't get a letter that reads like this: "Dear Josie, how do you put a nice glaze on roast chicken, duck, turkey, and ham?" It's always my pleasure to inform these gals that there are more ways than one to get a professional glaze on a roast.

If ham is to be served hot, the glaze has to be baked on. When the roast is taken out of the oven some kind of mixture high in sugar is spread all over the meat. Marmalade, honey, corn syrup or molasses, brown or granulated sugar can be used. To give the meat a tang, first spread the ham with prepared mustard, then the marmalade. Return the ham to a moderately hot oven for about 20 minutes until it's beautifully glazed. A sweet glaze naturally goes best with ham. For poultry, where you don't want a very sweet glaze, baste during the last half hour of roasting time with a mixture of honey or syrup and enough bottled gravy sauce to make it a rich brown. Not enough syrup will remain on the roast to make it taste sweet.

When you want to put a rich glaze on a cold roast for the buffet table—cold roast ham, turkey, chicken, beef, or veal

—you can do several things: either coat it with a clear glaze, or cover it completely with colored mayonnaise to which you have added a little dissolved gelatine. Let's take the clear glaze first. That's made of bouillon and gelatine. Start with an envelope of plain unflavored gelatine softened in a quarter cupful of cold water and then dissolve it in a cupful of heated undiluted canned bouillon. Let that get cold until it is as thick as unbeaten egg white, then paint it on with a brush. Yes, paint a layer of this mixture over the chilled roast. Put the roast back in the refrigerator and let glaze set. It only takes a few minutes for such a thin layer to firm; take it out and give it another coating. Put it back in the refrigerator until glaze firms. Do this until the coating is about, oh . . . five or six layers deep. You will be surprised at the beautiful gloss. After the final coating is set, it can be decorated with little cutouts of pimiento—using fancy cutters—or strips of pimiento and strips of green pepper or anything that you fancy, such as slices of stuffed olives. This is fun!

Here's a trick for decorating cold cooked hams that you'll love using—slightly tinted mayonnaise with gelatine and decalcomanias. Decalcomanias, or decals, are found in stationery and five-and-ten cent stores. They are easily applied. Pictures of animals, birds, and flowers on the decals are made to order for decorating hams for a buffet table. Using a large decalcomania on top of a big ham with a border of small ones around the sides gives a striking effect.

Allow 2 cups mayonnaise and 2 envelopes plain unflavored gelatine for a 10 to 12 pound ham. Tint the mayonnaise and warm it over hot water. Soften the gelatine in ½ cup cold water in a cup. Stand the cup in hot water until the gelatine is dissolved. Stir into the mayonnaise. Spread smoothly over the entire cold ham. Chill until the mayonnaise is firm and glossy. Soak the decals in warm water until loosened; smooth a large decal on top and several small ones around the ham sides. The decals cling nicely. They can be peeled off before slicing. Cold roasted turkeys decorated this way are perfectly beautiful. I did this demonstration on television and it created much excitement. The phones rang for hours for further instructions. Most viewers were surprised to learn that decorating meats for buffets could be so easy.

FRESH HAM STEAK SMOTHERED WITH SAUERKRAUT

Sauerkraut lovers, this is one of your dishes for sure! Fresh ham and sauerkraut are a natural. Here you can enjoy the combination without having to roast a large fresh ham, because you're working with just the fresh ham steaks. This is the sort of food combination you like to serve when it's cold outside with snow on the ground. It belongs to the old fashioned "stick-to-your-ribs" category of dishes. And don't discount the caraway seeds—they season the sauerkraut. At any rate, this is a dish worth making.

2½ to 3 lbs. thick fresh ham steak, cut into 6 pieces
3 tablespoons flour
1 teaspoon salt
¼ teaspoon ground black pepper
1 large onion, chopped
2 celery tops, chopped
2 cups water
¼ cup cider vinegar
1 can (1 lb.) sauerkraut (use 1 lb. 11 oz. can sauerkraut for sauerkraut lovers)
3 tablespoons brown sugar
2 teaspoons whole caraway seed
Salt to taste

Trim fat from meat; cut fat into small pieces; place fat in Dutch oven over low heat; cook, stirring frequently, 8 to 10 minutes or until crispy. Mix together flour, salt, and pepper. Rub into meat; place meat in fat in Dutch oven. Raise heat; cook about 10 to 12 minutes, turning frequently, until browned. Add onion, celery, water, vinegar. Cover and simmer over low heat about 1½ to 2 hours or until meat is tender. Add sauerkraut, brown sugar, caraway seed, and salt, to taste. Cover and simmer about ½ hour. Serve meat on platter surrounded by sauerkraut. Makes 6 to 8 servings.

◆§ ROAST LOIN OF PORK FLORIDIAN

Here's a dressed-up version of roast loin of pork to intrigue you. Succulent roast pork is one of the finest meats you could ever serve. But primped up like this it has new glamor. On TV this is what my comment was: "It's the same familiar roast pork with new trimmings. Trim your meats with the same idea you have in mind when you trim a new hat for Easter. The idea—fetching!"

- 1 unpeeled, thin-skinned, orange, sliced ¼" thick
- 1½ cups water
- 3 to 4 lbs. loin of pork
- 1 teaspoon salt
- ¼ teaspoon ground pepper
- ½ teaspoon ground sage leaves
- 15 whole cloves
- ½ teaspoon powdered dry mustard
- ¼ cup brown sugar
- ½ cup orange juice
- 1 to 1½ cups boiling water
- Salt and ground black papper to taste

Simmer sliced orange in water, covered, about 15 minutes or until rind is tender. Drain and set aside. Rub pork with salt, pepper, and sage; place on rack in open shallow pan. Place cooked orange slices on top of meat; anchor them to meat with toothpicks. Stud with cloves. Mix together mustard and brown sugar; sprinkle over orange and meat.

Moisten sugar with 2 to 3 teaspoons of orange juice. Bake in a slow oven (325°F.) about 2½ to 3 hours or until done, allowing 45 minutes per pound roasting time. Baste 3 to 4 times with orange juice during baking. Remove meat to serving platter. Pour fat out of roasting pan. Pour 1 to 1½ cups boiling water into pan. Boil 4 to 5 minutes, stirring brown particles off pan into liquid. Season with salt and pepper to taste. Strain gravy and pass with meat. Makes 6 to 8 servings.

❧ BAKED STUFFED PORK TENDERLOIN

After several requests on how to cook fresh pork tenderloin, this recipe made its bow on TV. The crew said it tasted mighty good—and why not, for pork tenderloin is the filet mignon of the pork and a great delicacy. We serve beef filet mignon rare, but since we never serve pork rare, "roasting to a turn" is the best treatment for pork tenderloin—and this recipe is superb.

- 2 cups soft bread crumbs
- 1 clove garlic, mashed
- 1 teaspoon whole marjoram leaves
- 1 teaspoon whole sage leaves, crumbled
- 1 tablespoon prepared horseradish
- 1 tablespoon melted butter or margarine
- ¼ cup fruit juice, any kind
- 2 (1 lb. each) fresh pork tenderloins
- Salt and ground black pepper
- 1½ cups chicken bouillon
- 1 tablespoon cornstarch
- ¼ cup cold water

Mix together crumbs, garlic, marjoram, sage, horseradish, butter, and fruit juice to make stuffing. Split tenderloins lengthwise along one side; spread open. Sprinkle with salt and pepper. Spread stuffing lengthwise along one half of each tenderloin; fold sides together. Skewer or tie closed with string. Place in greased shallow baking dish. Add bouillon. Cover and bake in a moderate oven (350°F.) about 45 minutes. Uncover, and bake about 30 to 40 minutes longer, or until cooked and lightly browned. Remove skewers or string; slice meat and place on serving platter. Pour pan gravy into small saucepan; bring to a boil. Mix together cornstarch and water; gradually add to gravy in saucepan, stirring rapidly; cook until slightly thickened and smooth, stirring constantly. Serve over sliced meat. Makes 4 servings.

CITY CHICKEN

4 to 5 thick pork loin chops
¾ lb. cubed lean boneless veal
½ teaspoon salt
Ground black pepper
Flour
¼ cup fat or oil
½ cup pineapple juice
¼ cup water
2 to 4 tablespoons chopped onion
6 short wooden or metal skewers

Trim fat and bones from chops. Cut lean pork into 1 to 1½-inch cubes. Fill small skewers with alternating cubes of veal and pork (allow about 4 meat cubes to each skewer). Sprinkle skewered meat evenly with salt, pepper, and flour. Heat fat in chicken fryer or skillet over moderate heat. Add skewered meat. Cook about 15 minutes or until evenly browned, turning frequently. Add pineapple juice, water, and chopped onion. Cover and simmer over very low heat about 1¼ hours, or until tender. (Add a few drops of water if needed.) Serve on skewers, allowing 1 skewer per serving. Makes 6 servings.

NOTE: Cook pork bones with dry beans for soup or with cabbage.

◆§ PICKLED PIGS' FEET IN JELLY

(Dedicated with love to Nick Kenny)

6 fresh pigs' feet, split in half lengthwise
2 quarts water
1 tablespoon salt
5 cups water
1 pint white vinegar
2 teaspoons salt
2 teaspoons sugar
¼ teaspoon whole cloves
¼ teaspoon peppercorns
1 bay leaf

Wash and drain pigs' feet. Place in kettle with water and salt; cover and simmer ½ hour. Drain, discarding the boiling water; rinse feet in cold water. Return feet to same kettle; add water, vinegar, salt, sugar, cloves, peppercorns, and bay leaf. Cover and simmer 3½ to 4 hours or until meat is tender but not falling off the bones. Lift out cooked feet; place into deep serving dish; strain broth over the feet. Cool, and chill until jellied. Makes 6 servings.

NOTE: If you like the feet boneless, do this: allow feet to cook until meat falls off bones: lift them out; remove and discard the bones. Place boneless meat into deep serving dish; cover with strained hot broth; cool and chill.

◆§ PORK CHOPS SINGAPORE

(by Eliot Elisofon—*Life* Photographer)

I did not know that Mr. Elisofon was going to be my guest until one half hour before show time. Someone had ordered in some extra food props which turned out to be pork chops and ginger. By now I'm so used to strange things in the studio that I wouldn't even bat a lash if a crated alligator were wheeled in. A prop to me today is a part of the everyday setup and those pork chops, I thought, would be used for some demonstration connected with me. I was not too surprised to learn that the guest was going to cook for *me*. Mr. Elisofon was a charming guest. He showed an artistic appreciation of food and handled the fry pan professionally. The pork chops were simply delicious, but then he is, after all, a finished artist, and *Life* is indebted to him for some of its most distinctive photography. So it all adds up. It takes artistry to develop a fine dish.

- 4 center-cut pork chops, 1 inch thick
- 1 clove garlic
- 1 teaspoon salt
- ¼ teaspoon ground black pepper
- 1 teaspoon ground ginger
- 4 to 5 tablespoons brown sugar
- 2 to 3 tablespoons wine vinegar
- ½ cup canned crushed pineapple

Brown the pork chops on both sides in a dry large skillet or frying pan, about 15 to 18 minutes. Mash together the garlic, salt, pepper, ginger, and sugar in a mortar. Add vinegar and blend. Add garlic mixture to chops. Lower the heat, cover and cook about 20 minutes or until meat is done, turning once. Spread crushed pineaple on chops; heat 5 to 6 minutes and serve. Makes 4 servings.

◆§ BARBECUED SPARERIBS

- 1 clove garlic, mashed
- ½ cup soy sauce
- ¼ cup honey
- 1 tablespoon wine vinegar
- ¼ cup fresh orange juice
- 1 teaspoon grated orange rind
- 1 teaspoon salt
- ½ teaspoon ground ginger
- ⅛ teaspoon ground black pepper
- 2½ to 3 lbs. fresh spareribs, cut into 2-rib pieces

Mix together garlic, soy sauce, honey, vinegar, orange juice, rind, salt, ginger, and pepper; pour mixture over spareribs. Mix thoroughly. Refrigerate uncovered for about 1 hour or longer, turning 3 to 4 times to get even distribution of sauce. Drain spareribs; place on broiler rack, reserving sauce. Broil about 7 to 9 inches from heat, about 1½ to 1¾ hours or until cooked and browned, turning spareribs every 10 minutes and basting with reserved sauce. Makes 4 servings.

◆§ ROAST STUFFED SPARERIBS WITH SAUSAGE FORCEMEAT STUFFING

This is one of the most popular of our meat dishes that we have done this year. Folks seemed to come out of the walls after the stuffed spareribs. They asked for bread and they went for stuffing—they used it as a sandwich filling. The men begged me for the recipe to take home to their wives. I sure wish you'd try this with veal sometime, because veal is so bland that it needs something spicy, and this is spicy. I guess a better word would be savory.

2 sets (5 to 6 lbs.) fresh spareribs
Salt and ground black pepper
Sausage Forcemeat Stuffing (see recipe on next page)
1 tablespoon molasses

Leave spareribs whole. Have bones at thick end cracked for easy slicing when roasted. Sprinkle lightly with salt and pepper. Cover hollowed side of one set of spareribs with stuffing. Cover with remaining spareribs. Skewer all around with poultry pins; lace closed with twine. Brush with molasses. Place on rack in shallow open pan in slow oven (325°F.) and bake about 2½ to 2¾ hours or until ribs and stuffing are done, turning once. Serve sliced. Makes 6 to 8 servings.

Sausage Forcemeat Stuffing

1 lb. fresh pork sausage meat
½ lb. ground lean veal
2 cups soft bread crumbs
¼ cup minced onion
¼ cup minced parsley
3 egg whites
½ cup thick cream sauce or undiluted canned celery or mushroom soup
1 teaspoon salt

Combine pork sausage, veal, bread crumbs, onion, parsley, egg whites, cream sauce, and salt in mixing bowl. Beat 5 to 6 minutes by hand or about 3 minutes at medium speed of mixer. Use as stuffing for spareribs, stuffed breast of veal, shoulder of veal, or poultry. Makes about 4 cups.

◆§ FIESTA CHAFING DISH SPARERIB APPETIZERS

3 lbs. fresh spareribs, cut into bite-sized portions
1½ cups boiling water
½ cup tomato sauce
1 cup moist mincemeat
5 to 6 drops bottled hot sauce

Place ribs in dry large skillet or frying pan over moderate heat. Cook slowly about 40 minutes or until evenly browned, turning occasionally. Transfer browned ribs to shallow open pan. Pour out all fat from skillet. Add water to skillet, stirring to dissolve brown bits in pan; pour over browned ribs. Mix together tomato sauce, mincemeat, and hot sauce; pour over ribs in pan. Cover and bake in a moderate oven (350°F.) about ½ hour. Uncover and bake about 30 to 45 minutes or until done and nicely browned. Transfer to chafing dish and keep hot. Makes 6 to 8 servings.

BAKED BLACK-EYED PEAS AND SPARERIBS

2 cups dry black-eyed peas
1 quart cold water
2 tablespoons ketchup
1 onion, finely chopped
1 tablespoon salt
2 lbs. fresh spareribs, cut into serving pieces
1 teaspoon salt
¼ teaspoon ground black pepper
½ cup molasses

Pick over and wash peas. Soak in 1 quart cold water about 2 hours. Drain and measure the water; add more water if needed to make 1 quart. Combine peas, water, ketchup, onion, salt, and spareribs in saucepan. Cover and simmer about ½ hour. Turn into greased shallow casserole. Rub spareribs with salt and pepper; brush with molasses. Place meat over peas; add any remaining molasses. Cover and bake in a slow oven (325°F.) about 1½ hours or until meat and peas are tender. Uncover and bake about ½ hour longer or until meat is browned, turning 2 or 3 times for even browning. Serve with hot spoon bread. Makes 6 to 8 servings.

ROAST SUCKLING PIG WITH HERBED APPLE CIDER STUFFING

12 lb. dressed suckling pig
1½ teaspoons salt
¼ teaspoon ground black pepper
⅛ teaspoon garlic powder
Herbed Apple Cider Stuffing
2 tablespoons melted butter or margarine
2 cups boiling water
Roast Suckling Pig Gravy
1 fresh, small red apple
2 maraschino cherries
Fresh cranberries, strung to make necklace for pig's neck
Spiced crabapples for garnish
⅓ cup brandy

Wash suckling pig in cold water and wipe dry. Mix salt, pepper, and garlic powder together. Rub mixture on insides of pig. Stuff pig loosely with Herbed Apple Cider Stuffing (see below). Close opening in body with skewer fastening. Wipe the outside of the skin and rub with melted butter or margarine. Place a small block of wood in the pig's mouth to brace it for the apple which will be inserted later. Place pig, in kneeling position, on a rack in a large open shallow pan. Pour 2 cups boiling water in pan and cover loosely with alminum foil. Roast in a slow oven (325°F.) about 5 hours or until tender, basting every 3/4 hour with hot water in the pan. Add more water as necessary. Remove pig to large serving platter. Make Roast Suckling Pig Gravy (see below). Replace wooden block with a small red apple. Insert a large maraschino cherry in each eye socket. Place a cranberry necklace around the pig's neck. Garnish platter with spiced crabapples, if desired. Heat brandy in ladle; touch a lighted match to it and pour flaming over pig at the table. Serve with heated gravy. Makes 12 servings.

Herbed Apple Cider Stuffing

3 quarts toasted bread cubes
¾ cup dried onion flakes
¼ cup dried parsley flakes
1½ teaspoons whole thyme leaves, crumbled
1 tablespoon whole celery seed
1 tablespoon salt
¼ teaspoon ground black pepper
½ cup melted butter or margarine,
1 cup apple cider

Combine toasted bread cubes, dried onion flakes, dried parsley flakes, thyme, celery seed, salt, and pepper. Stir in butter and cider; mix lightly. Stuff pig loosely. Close opening of pig's body cavity with skewers and lacing. Bake as in above directions.

Roast Suckling Pig Gravy

Measure the fat in the suckling pig roasting pan. There should be about 1/3 cup. Pour it back into the pan and heat. Add 2 1/2 cups hot water or bouillon and stir with a wooden spoon to loosen brown portion sticking to bottom of the pan. Blend 1/3 cup flour to a smooth paste with 1/2 cup cold water; gradually add to pan. Cook until gravy has reached the desired thickness. Stir in 1 teaspoon salt, 1/16 teaspoon ground black pepper, and 1/16 teaspoon garlic powder. Serve hot, over meat and stuffing. Makes approximately 2 1/2 cups.

❧ PIGS' TROTTERS, SWEET AND SOUR

This is a man's dish—but women like it too. In searching around for something a little different to have on your buffet table for a party, why not try Pigs' Trotters, Sweet and Sour? They're mighty good. Of course, there's not much to eat on pig's feet, but then mostly it's their flavor people relish and the bones they love to "chew on." I guess you'd say this is a dish with a Chinese flavor.

6 fresh pigs' feet, split in half
Boiling water
2 teaspoons salt
Flour
4 to 6 tablespoons oil
2 cups cider vinegar
1 cup brown sugar
2 cloves garlic, mashed
1 tablespoon chopped preserved ginger
1½ cups water

Wash feet in hot water, then in cold water; drain. Place in saucepan; cover with boiling water. Add salt. Cover and simmer about 2 hours or until partly cooked. Drain; spread out to dry. Coat with flour. Heat oil in skillet or frying pan; add floured pigs' feet; cook about 10 to 15 minutes, or until browned, turning frequently. Lift out; drain on absorbent paper. Mix together vinegar, brown sugar, garlic, ginger, and water in kettle or saucepan. Add browned pigs' feet; cover and simmer about 2 hours or until tender but slightly chewy, turning several times during cooking. Add a small amount of water as needed if meat cooks dry. Serve hot or cold. Makes 6 servings.

NOTE: These can be cut into 4 pieces before cooking, and then they become a finger food.

ITALIAN EASTER SAUSAGE PIE

The reason this recipe got on television was by popular request. When the calls came in for me to make this pie I was at a complete loss because I had never even seen it, let alone heard of it. One viewer remarked that I had been successful in tracking down two or three real Italian recipes for her, so could I please track down the Italian Easter Sausage Pie? Track it down I did—but it took me about three months. Fortunately, the requests came early enough in the season so that I was ready for the Easter week demonstration. I even enlisted the aid of Enrico Cortese, an NBC make-up artist whose sister-in-law was a grand cook, ran an Italian-American delicatessen in New Jersey, and made her own pastry. He brought me in a baked sausage pie. What with having unearthed three rather vague recipes for this delicacy and having an actual pie to analyze, it wasn't difficult to make. The pie was considered wonderful.

1 lb. fresh-type Italian sausage
4 eggs, beaten
½ cup milk
¾ cup diced mozarella cheese
½ cup grated Parmesan cheese
¼ cup shelled pine nuts
½ teaspoon salt
1 recipe pastry for 2-crust pie

Dice and cook sausage in dry skillet over moderate heat until fat flows. Drain; set aside and discard fat. Combine eggs and milk; add mozarella and Parmesan cheese, pine nuts, and salt. Add cooled cooked sausage. Line a 9-inch pie plate with pastry; add filling and moisten lower rim with water. Cover with rolled-out top crust. Trim edges one inch beyond edge of plate; seal and flute all around. Make several slits near center to allow escape of steam. Brush top with milk. Bake in a moderate oven (375°F.) 55 minutes to 1 hour. Cool on rack. Makes 1 pie—6 to 8 servings.

☙ SHORT RIBS OF BEEF WITH SAUERKRAUT

2 to 3 lbs. beef short ribs, cut into serving-sized pieces
1½ teaspoons salt
½ teaspoon ground black pepper
1 cup water
1 can (1 lb. 11 oz.) sauerkraut
1 small onion, sliced
2 tablespoons flour
¼ cup water

Place meat in Dutch oven or kettle over moderate heat; cook 12 to 15 minutes or until evenly browned, turning pieces over frequently. Pour off drippings. Add salt and pepper. Add water; lower heat. Cover and simmer 2 to 2½ hours or until tender. Add sauerkraut and onion. Cover and simmer 30 to 35 minutes or until flavors have blended; remove meat to hot platter. Mix together flour and water until smooth; add to sauerkraut, stirring constantly; cover and simmer 2 to 3 minutes or until slightly thickened. Serve kraut around meat. Makes 4 to 6 servings.

POTTED STUFFED CUBE STEAKS

3 tablespoons butter or margarine
1 cup minced celery leaves
1 cup chopped onion
¼ cup minced parsley
4 pimientos, chopped
2 cups soft bread crumbs
½ teaspoon ground sage leaves
1 teaspoon salt
¼ teaspoon ground black pepper
6 (1½ lbs.) cube beef steaks
3 tablespoons butter or margarine
¾ cup tomato juice
Water

Heat butter or margarine in large skillet or frying pan over moderate heat; add celery, onion, and parsley; cook about 8 to 10 minutes, or until soft, stirring often. Remove from heat; add pimientos, bread crumbs, sage, salt, and pepper; mix well. Spread mixture over steaks to within ¾-inch of edges. Roll up and skewer or tie in place. Heat butter or margarine in large skillet or frying pan over high heat; add steaks; cook about 6 to 8 minutes, turning over repeatedly until evenly browned. Add tomato juice; lower heat; cover tightly and simmer about 1¼ hours, or until tender, turning meat once. Add water during cooking if needed. Serve with unthickened pan gravy. Makes 6 servings.

BORDEAUX BEEF STEW

2 lbs. round steak, cut into 1-inch cubes
2 bacon slices, diced
2 medium onions, chopped
2 tablespoons butter or margarine
2 tablespoons flour
1 cup red Bordeaux wine
1 cup consomme
1 carrot, sliced
1 bay leaf
¼ teaspoon whole thyme leaves
1 teaspoon salt
10 small fresh onions
½ cup sliced mushrooms
6 small hot boiled potatoes

Brown meat, bacon, and onions in hot butter or margarine in Dutch oven or large kettle. Add flour. Stir constantly about 5 to 6 minutes, or until browned. Add wine, consomme, carrot, bay leaf, thyme, and salt. Cover and simmer about 2 hours, or until meat is tender. Add onions and mushrooms. Cover and simmer 40 to 45 minutes longer or until onions are tender. Serve with hot boiled potatoes. Makes 6 servings.

DRIED BEEF HELENE

Boiling water
1½ cups diced dried beef
3 tablespoons butter or margarine
1 tablespoon flour
½ teaspoon paprika
¼ teaspoon ground nutmeg
½ teaspoon Worcestershire sauce
1½ cups milk
1 cup canned sliced mushrooms
¼ cup sliced ripe olives
Buttered toast

Pour boiling water to cover over dried beef; drain. Melt butter or margarine in large skillet or frying pan; add flour, paprika, nutmeg, and Worcestershire sauce; stir. Gradually add milk, stirring until smooth and thickened. Add dried beef and mushrooms; cook, stirring frequently, about 5 to 6 minutes or until mushrooms and beef are heated throughout. Add olives. Serve on hot buttered toast. Makes 4 servings.

JINX McCRARY'S FAVORITE RECIPE

When I asked Jinx for her favorite recipe, I fully expected her to say "Chicken Breast Under Glass—or Pressed Duck." What a surprise I had when she gave me this. On first hearing about it, I thought it a plebeian concoction.

Knowing Jinx, it's perfectly evident to me that she has very little time to spend in the kitchen with all her outside obligations. She must be a good manager. The fact that she has chosen a recipe like this, which puts the burden of work on the packer of the food, shows that she *is* a good manager. Outside of peeling and mashing the garlic and straining the tomatoes, all this recipe requires is the opening of cans. I venture to guess, notwithstanding all the help that Jinx McCrary must have in her household, that once in a while she is followed home by a group—a hungry group, that is—who expects to be fed. This is exactly the kind of a situation that will make this dish a five-star special.

The flavor of the dish is slightly sophisticated. It looks sophisticated—and yet it's everyday. It all adds up—that you can serve it to anybody, even to people who are used to eating in great restaurants like Maxim's in Paris, or in the Automat. As I said before, this dish is very little work, and yet it represents a lot of work somewhere by someone. For instance, those tamales. That's half a day's work for an experienced Mexican cook. Then the roast beef. Somebody had to buy the beef, roast it—by the way, this can be bought canned—and make the gravy (this too can be bought canned). Somebody had to can the corn, somebody had to cure and can the olives, and somebody had to produce and pack the raisins. So the work is there, but it doesn't have to be done by the cook who presents the dish—that's the beauty of it. I wish you'd try it for a crowd. It's terrific! I taught it to a bachelor who entertains and cooks for his numerous guests, and he found it so successful that he's used it now for two years running. Jinx told me her mother gave her the recipe, so we'll have to pin a bouquet on Jinx's mother for this unusual, helpful party creation. Naturally, while it's baking you could toss a salad, and if you thought to buy some French bread you could turn it into garlic bread—and there's your meal.

2 cups diced cold roast beef
2 cups canned or left-over beef gravy
2 cans (1 lb. each) or jars tamales
2 cans (12 oz. each) whole kernel corn
1 can (9 oz.) whole small black olives, drained
2 cups raisins
3 cups canned tomatoes
1 clove garlic, mashed

Combine roast beef and gravy. Add tamales, which have been cut into 1-inch pieces. Add corn, olives, and raisins. Rub tomatoes through coarse sieve to remove seeds, then add with garlic. Mix thoroughly. Turn into large roasting pan or into 2 deep casseroles. Bake uncovered in a slow oven (300°F.) about 2 hours. Serve with a mixed green salad and garlic bread or fresh Cuban bread. This dish can wait for hours. Makes 12 to 14 servings.

☙ CORNED BEEF GLACE

5 lbs. corned beef brisket
Water to cover
1 cup brown sugar
1 tablespoon flour
1 teaspoon powdered dry mustard
¼ cup vinegar
Whole cloves

Place meat in kettle or Dutch oven. Cover completely with water. Place over high heat. Bring to boiling temperature. Lower heat; cover and simmer 4 to 5 hours or until tender. Lift cooked meat out of liquid; place fat-side-up on rack in open pan. Reserve liquid to cook greens for accompaniment. Mix together brown sugar, flour, mustard, and vinegar, stirring until smooth. Spread over cooked corned beef. Stud meat with cloves. Place in a moderate oven

(350°F.) about 20 to 25 minutes or until shiny and glazed. Makes 10 to 12 servings.

NOTE: Serve with baked or boiled potatoes and cabbage or kale, onions, carrots, or turnips, cooked in some of the corned beef liquid.

CORNED BEEF HASH

- 1 cup chopped onion
- 4 tablespoons corned beef fat, butter, or margarine
- 2 cups chopped cooked corned beef
- 2 cups chopped cooked potatoes
- Freshly ground black pepper
- Salt, if needed

Combine onion and fat in large skillet or frying pan. Place over medium heat; cook until onions are soft and lightly browned, stirring often; remove from heat. Combine onions, corned beef, potatoes, and pepper. Add salt if needed. Mix well. Shape into 4 large or 6 medium patties. Heat large dry heavy skillet over moderate heat; add patties without crowding. Cook until crispy undercrust forms. Turn with pancake turner and brown other side. Serve piping hot. Excellent with poached eggs on top. Makes 4 to 6 servings.

ACORN SQUASH STUFFED WITH HASH

- 2 medium-sized acorn squash, unpared
- Salt
- 2 cups beef or canned beef hash
- ½ cup ketchup
- 4 bacon slices

Cut acorn squash lengthwise into halves. Scoop out seeds. Place squash in colander over boiling water; cover and steam 5 to 7 minutes. Remove from water. Salt squash lightly. Pack hash with rounded top into the hollows of the squash, and coat lightly with ketchup. Cover with slices of bacon cut into halves. Bake in a moderate oven (375°F.) about 45 minutes, or until squash is tender and bacon crisped. Makes 4 servings.

❧ TOP-OF-THE-STOVE MEAT LOAF

Everyone was quizzical when I declared the television "Dish of the Day" would be meat loaf—done on top of the stove, not in the oven. Of course, I knew it was going to be good because I had tested it and served it in my own home to guests. The day I made this on television the usual excitement about "What are you making today, Josie?" died down at the selection of meat loaf. I've always maintained that a meat loaf can be extraordinarily good eating. Well, would you like to know what the studio verdict of the top-of-the-stove meat loaf was? I could have served three or four more to the gang after the show was over.

Many complaints in the mail concern meat loaf. How do you make a meat loaf that tastes like something? How do you make a meat loaf that sticks together? How do you make a meat loaf that isn't hard on the outside and still moist in the middle? That's the general tone of the letters I get about meat loaf. This loaf is round—the shape of a round loaf of pumpernickel. It's served cut in wedges. It slices like a dream, hangs together but still is moist, and has a fine flavor. There's a nice balance of seasonings in the mixture and of course the ketchup adds flavor. Don't expect it to have a brown crust, since it is steam cooked. When we did this on television we got thousands of requests for the recipe.

- 1½ lbs. ground beef chuck
- ½ lb. ground fresh lean pork
- 2 cups soft bread crumbs
- 1 medium green pepper, chopped
- ¾ cup ketchup
- 2 eggs, beaten
- 2 teaspoons ground celery seed
- 2 teaspoons salt
- ⅛ teaspoon ground black pepper
- 2 tablespoons prepared mustard
- 2 slices bacon, cut in half
- ¼ cup ketchup

Combine beef, pork, bread crumbs, green pepper, ketchup, eggs, celery seed, salt, pepper, and mustard. Mix thoroughly. Roll into round loaf. Place bacon on bottom of 8-inch pie pan. Place shaped meat loaf over bacon. Spread outside of meat loaf evenly with remaining ketchup. Place in steamer (see note). Cover and steam about 2 hours. Serve with a mushroom or celery sauce. Makes 6 to 8 servings.

NOTE: To steam in Dutch oven or large kettle, place rack in the bottom of the pot; add boiling water just up to the rack and stand pie pan on rack. Cover tightly and boil gently, regulating heat to keep water simmering, and adding more water as it boils away.

BEEF STEW AND DUMPLINGS

- 1½ lbs. boned chuck, cut into 1½-inch cubes
- 1 teaspoon caraway seed
- 2 cups boiling water
- 2 to 3 teaspoons salt
- ¾ cup diced celery
- ¾ cup diced white turnips
- ¾ cup sliced carrots
- 1 cup diced onions
- 1 cup diced potatoes
- ¼ teaspoon ground black pepper
- 2 teaspoons flour
- ¼ cup cold water

Brown meat in its own fat with caraway seed in Dutch oven, about 10 to 15 minutes. Add boiling water and salt. Cover and simmer about 1½ to 2 hours until barely tender.

Add celery, turnips, carrots, and onions. Simmer 15 minutes. Add potatoes. Cover and simmer until vegetables are tender but unbroken. Add pepper. Stir flour into cold water, then stir into boiling stew. Drop tablespoonfuls of dumpling batter (recipe below) on top of stew. Cover and simmer about 15 minutes. Serve at once on heated platter with stew in center. Makes 4 servings.

Dumplings for Stew

2 cups sifted all-purpose flour
3½ teaspoons double-acting baking powder
1 teaspoon salt
2 teaspoons shortening
1 cup milk

Sift together flour, baking powder, and salt into mixing bowl. Add shortening; rub in or blend until like fine meal. Add milk all at once and mix lightly to form soft dough. Cook dumplings in stew as above.

SMOKED BEEF TONGUE

Meaty smoked beef tongues come in 2- to 5-pound weights. Cooking tongue is simplicity itself. Merely cover the tongue with cold water and bring to a boil; reduce heat and simmer until fork-tender, usually 1 to 1¼ hours per pound. A medium-sized tongue takes from 3 to 3½ hours cooking. Nothing needs to be added. No particular cooking skill is required to provide one of the most savory sandwich fillings or cold cut platter favorites. No particular knack is required to peel off the tough protective rind from the cooked tongue or to cut away the root ends and fatty portion. Cooling the tongue in the cooking water gives a plumper, moister product.

Sliced across, as thick as you like, cooked tongue, served

hot with spinach or other greens, is a favorite with the male set and relished by many women. Cooked tongue is rich, savory and versatile. It can be served for breakfast or brunch, teamed with scrambled or fried eggs. Sliced tongue cooked in an egg pancake is excellent! Smoked cooked tongue is superb in casserole combinations such as tongue and spaghetti, tongue and green peas, in cheese sauce, or tongue and rice or lima beans. Smoked tongue belongs in salads too. What would chef's salad bowl be without its characteristic strips of tender smoked tongue? Diced tongue and celery or other crispy salad vegetables make a superb summer main dish salad, just by combining with a snappy French dressing. A portion of smoked tongue in the refrigerator means that makings for sandwiches, salads, hot dishes, and even appetizers are yours for having remembered that smoked tongue is one of your staunchest allies.

◆§ BEEF TONGUE ORIENTALE

1 (3 to 4 lbs.) smoked beef tongue
Cold water to cover
3 to 4 slices onion
1 clove garlic, crushed
2 bay leaves
2 tablespoons vinegar
2 tablespoons brown sugar
2 tablespoons honey
1 cup raisins
6 crushed gingersnaps
1 tablespoon cornstarch
¼ cup cold water

Place tongue and water in large kettle or Dutch oven; add onion, garlic, and bay leaves; bring to boiling temperature; cover and simmer 2 hours. Lift out tongue; remove skin and root ends. Strain liquid and return 4 cupfuls to kettle. Skim off fat (easily done by floating outside lettuce leaves in broth and then discarding them with clinging fat). Add trimmed tongue, vinegar, sugar, honey, and raisins. Cover and simmer about 1 to 1½ hours or until tender. Mix together gingersnaps, cornstarch, and cold water; stir into broth. Simmer about 5 minutes, or until broth is slightly thickened and smooth. Lift out tongue and place onto serving platter. Serve sauce on top and on the side. Makes 12 servings.

BEEF TONGUE IN ASPIC

2 envelopes plain unflavored gelatine
½ cup cold water
1 can (10½ oz.) hot condensed consomme
½ teaspoon salt
¼ cup vinegar
6 slices cooked smoked beef tongue
1 cup coarsely chopped cooked smoked beef tongue
½ cup diced celery
2 tablespoons grated horseradish
⅛ teaspoon ground black pepper
⅓ cup diced pimiento

Sprinkle gelatine on cold water in cup to soften. Stand cup in boiling water, until gelatine is thoroughly dissolved; add to hot consomme, stirring briskly. Add salt and vinegar, mixing until blended. Pour ¼ cup of the consomme mixture into bottom of a 6-cup mold or loaf pan; chill 5 to 6 minutes or until firm. Overlap sliced tongue in bottom of mold on firmed consomme; pour ¼ cup of the consomme mixture over sliced tongue, chilling again until firm. Meanwhile, mix together remaining consomme mixture, chopped tongue, celery, horseradish, pepper, and pimiento until blended; spoon into mold over sliced tongue. Refrigerate several hours, or overnight. Unmold and serve sliced. Makes 6 servings.

OXTAIL RAGOUT

2 large (4 to 5 lbs.) oxtails, cut in pieces at joints
¼ to ⅓ cup flour
3 tablespoons butter or margarine
1 cup canned tomatoes
1½ cup bouillon (use bouillon cube)
2 stalks celery, cut across into 1-inch pieces
1 clove garlic, sliced
1 bay leaf
3 to 4 whole cloves
2 teaspoons salt
¼ teaspoon ground black pepper
4 carrots, diced
2 large onions, cut into quarters
1 small potato, peeled and grated

Quickly rinse oxtails in boiling water, then in cold water; drain and pat dry. Coat with flour. Heat butter or margarine in Dutch oven or kettle over moderate heat until frothy. Add oxtails; cook until browned, turning repeatedly. Add tomatoes, bouillon, celery, garlic, bay leaf, cloves, salt, and pepper. Cover and simmer 3 to 4 hours, or until fork-tender. Remove from heat; let stand until fat rises to surface; skim off fat. Return oxtails to cook over moderate heat; add carrots and onions. Cover and simmer ½ hour or until vegetables are tender. Add grated potato, stirring until gravy is slightly thickened. Cook 2 to 3 minutes. Makes 4 servings.

COLD SPICED BOILED BEEF FLANK

2 quarts boiling water
1 large onion, sliced
2 stalks celery, sliced
1 carrot, sliced
2 cloves garlic, sliced
2 tablespoons sugar
2 to 3 bay leaves
6 whole cloves
1 tablespoon salt
6 to 8 peppercorns
2 tablespoons vinegar
3 to 3½ lbs. beef flank or plate, in one piece
Grated horseradish
Prepared mustard

Place water, onion, celery, carrot, garlic, sugar, bay leaves, cloves, salt, peppercorns, and vinegar in Dutch oven or large kettle over high heat. Boil uncovered 5 minutes. Add meat; lower heat; cover and simmer 3½ to 4 hours or until fork-tender, adding more water if needed during cooking. Remove from heat; let meat cool in broth. Remove meat. Slice across grain. Serve with horseradish and mustard. Makes 6 servings.

NOTE: Broth may be used for soup or gravies; trimmings may be used for hash.

◆§ COLD BOILED BRISKET OF BEEF

3½ to 5 lbs. fresh beef brisket
Hot water
1 peeled onion, studded with 6 to 7 whole cloves
2 cloves garlic
½ teaspoon peppercorns
1 sprig parsley
2 stalks celery, with leaves
½ cup white vinegar
2 tablespoons salt
Fresh grated horseradish

Place meat in Dutch oven or deep kettle. Add hot water to cover. Add onion, garlic, peppercorns, parsley, celery, vinegar, and salt. Cover. Place over high heat and bring to boiling temperature. Lower heat; cover and simmer 3½ to 4 hours or until meat is fork-tender. Cool meat in broth. Remove meat. Slice across the grain and serve with horseradish. Makes 8 servings.

NOTE: Broth may be used for stock or gravies.

SOUTHERN BEEF HASH

2 tablespoons salad oil or shortening
2 tablespoons chopped onion
2 cups diced potatoes
1 cup diced celery
½ cup diced green pepper
1 cup bouillon (use bouillon cube)
1 cup canned tomatoes
2 cups diced cooked beef
Salt and ground black pepper, to taste

Heat oil or shortening in saucepan over moderate heat. Add onions and cook 6 to 8 minutes or until lightly browned, stirring frequently. Add potatoes, celery, green pepper, bouillon, and tomatoes. Cover and simmer about 20 minutes or until potatoes are barely tender. Add beef, salt, and pepper; simmer 10 minutes or until done. Serve in soup bowls with hot corn bread. Makes 4 servings.

PLANKED SIRLOIN STEAK

3½ to 4 lbs. sirloin steak (1½"- to 1¾"-thick), trimmed of excess fat
Salt and ground black pepper
3 cups cold riced or mashed potatoes
3 egg yolks, beaten
¾ teaspoon salt
⅛ teaspoon ground black pepper
Melted butter or margarine
1 cup hot cooked seasoned peas
1 cup hot, cooked, seasoned whole kernel corn
1 cup hot, cooked, seasoned green beans
1 can (8-oz.) hot seasoned asparagus tips
2 small tomatoes, cut into halves and broiled
2 to 4 tablespoons melted butter or margarine
Radish roses and parsley sprigs

Slash fat around steak in several places, to keep steak from curling during broiling. Place steak on greased rack in broiler pan. Broil steak 3 inches from heat in pre-heated broiler 12 to 14 minutes (rare), or 15 to 17 minutes (medium-rare). Sprinkle with salt and pepper; turn over and broil 6 to 7 minutes. Meanwhile, mix together potatoes, egg yolks, salt, and pepper; beat until light; fill into cake decorating bag having large star tube attachment; set aside. Brush large "special planking" wooden plank with melted butter or margarine; heat in moderate oven (350°F.) 5 to 6 minutes or until heated through. Season top of steak with salt and pepper; place on plank. Dress a heavy border of potatoes through star tube around steak inside edge of plank; dress potato sections from steak to border, with spaces large enough to hold vegetables. Return steak to broiler. For rare steak broil 4 to 6 minutes or until steak is done and potatoes lightly browned. For medium-rare, lower the broiler pan so top of steak is 4 inches from heat; broil 8 to 10 minutes. Fill potato sections around steak with vegetables, arranging them colorfully. Brush steak and vegetables with butter or margarine and garnish with radish roses and parsley. Place plank on large napkin-lined platter. Serve from plank. Makes 4 servings.

STUFFED ROUND STEAK

2 lbs. round steak, cut ½-inch thick
1 teaspoon garlic salt
¼ teaspoon ground black pepper
1 cup cooked rice
½ cup chopped onion
¼ cup minced parsley
¼ cup grated carrot
2 tablespoons grated Parmesan cheese
½ teaspoon paprika
¼ cup claret
½ cup water
1 tablespoon ketchup
½ teaspoon salt
1 tablespoon flour
2 tablespoons soft butter or margarine

Sprinkle meat with garlic salt and pepper. Pound to one-half its original thickness; cut into 4 equal portions. Mix together rice, onion, parsley, carrot, cheese, and paprika. Spread evenly over meat; roll up; skewer or tie with string. Place in greased shallow casserole. Mix together claret, water, ketchup, and salt; pour over meat. Cover and bake in a moderate oven (350°F.) about 1 to 1½ hours or until tender. Uncover; bake about 20 to 25 minutes longer or until slightly browned. Remove skewers or string; place meat on serving platter. Pour pan gravy into small saucepan; place over moderate heat. Mix together flour and butter or margarine; stir until creamy. Add hot gravy to mixture, 2 tablespoons at a time, stirring until smooth. Return to saucepan; cook 3 to 4 minutes or until slightly thickened and smooth, stirring constantly. Pour over meat and serve. Makes 4 servings.

KOREAN CELESTIAL BEEF AND MUSHROOMS

½ to ¾ lb. ground beef chuck
2 tablespoons soy sauce
¼ cup minced onion
1 clove garlic, minced
½ teaspoon salt
⅛ teaspoon ground black pepper
1 tablespoon sesame seed (toasted in dry skillet or oven)
12 large mushroom caps
Flour
2 eggs, beaten
2 tablespoons water
3 to 4 tablespoons salad oil
½ cup water
1 tablespoon soy sauce
½ to ¾ teaspoon salt
1 teaspoon salad oil

Mix together beef, soy sauce, onion, garlic, salt, pepper, and toasted sesame seed; shape into 12 small flat patties. Slice mushroom caps across in half. Place one meat patty between each pair of mushroom halves; press together.

Coat mushroom-meat patties with flour. Mix together eggs and water. Dip patties in mixture; reserve any left-over egg. Heat oil in large skillet or frying pan; add patties; brown evenly, turning frequently. Add water, soy sauce, and salt; cover and simmer about 30 to 35 minutes, or until done and liquid has been absorbed. Heat oil in small skillet or frying pan; add reserved left-over egg; cook 2 to 3 minutes until firm, like a pancake. Roll pancake up tightly; slice across in thin shreds. Place cooked patties on warmed platter; sprinkle egg pancake shreds on top. Makes 4 servings.

BUTTERMILK POT ROAST

2 cups buttermilk
2 teaspoons salt
6 to 7 peppercorns
1 clove garlic, crushed
1 onion, chopped
2 to 3 bay leaves
3 to 4 lbs. boned chuck pot roast
3 tablespoons flour
3 tablespoons melted fat or oil
2 to 3 tablespoons commercial sour cream

Mix together buttermilk, salt, peppercorns, garlic, onion, and bay leaves. Pour over meat in deep bowl. Cover and refrigerate about 12 to 14 hours, turning two or three times during that period. To cook, drain meat and wipe dry. Strain and reserve liquid. Coat meat with flour. Heat fat in Dutch oven or kettle. Add meat and cook about 15 to 20 minutes or until browned, turning frequently. Add strained buttermilk mixture. Cover and simmer over low heat about 3½ to 4 hours or until fork-tender.* Remove meat to serving platter. Stir sour cream into pot juices and remove from heat at once. Serve over sliced meat. Makes 8 to 10 servings. (* If meat cooks dry, add a little water from time to time.)

BEEF AND CHILI BEAN POT

- 2 tablespoons salad oil, butter, or margarine
- 1 lb. ground chuck
- 1 cup diced onion
- 1 cup diced green pepper
- 2 cans (20-oz. each) red kidney beans and liquid
- 2 teaspoons salt
- 2 tablespoons chili powder
- ½ teaspoon ground oregano leaves
- ½ teaspoon ground black pepper
- 1 cup canned tomato sauce
- ½ cup cubed sharp Cheddar cheese
- Onion rings for garnish

Heat oil in large skillet or frying pan. Add meat, onion, and green pepper; cook about 12 to 15 minutes, or until browned, stirring frequently. Add kidney beans and liquid, salt, chili powder, oregano, pepper, tomato sauce, and cheese. Mix well. Turn into a 2½-quart bean pot. Cover and bake in a slow oven (325°F.) about 1 hour, or until done. Garnish top with raw onion rings and serve. Makes 6 to 8 servings.

GREEK MEAT BALLS IN EGG AND LEMON SAUCE

Every once in a while when you feel like some adventurous eating, a dish like this will strike your fancy. It's the same old hamburg or ground beef done up to be very important. It's unusually good, with a refreshing flavor as a result of the lemon juice. Serve it with broccoli or asparagus and either rice or some form of potatoes. I think you'll find Greek meat balls in egg and lemon sauce nice enough to serve to the club that you have to cook for in your own home once in a while. I mention this because the budgets for these occasions are usually pretty limited, and yet the women who come to lunch expect some surprise.

- 1 lb. ground beef, chuck or round
- 1½ cups cooked rice
- 2 tablespoons chopped parsley
- 1 small onion, chopped
- 1 tablespoon chopped fresh mint or 1 teaspoon mint flakes
- ½ teaspoon salt
- ½ teaspoon ground black pepper
- Flour
- 2 cups water
- 1 teaspoon salt
- 3 eggs, beaten
- 2 tablespoons fresh lemon juice

Combine beef, rice, parsley, onion, mint, salt and pepper; mix thoroughly and refrigerate ½ hour. Roll meat into egg-shaped balls. Coat with flour. Bring water and salt to boiling temperature in a saucepan or kettle. Add meat balls, a few at a time. Lower heat, cover and simmer about 45 minutes, or until cooked. Strain broth off meat, reserving the broth. Combine eggs and lemon juice, mixing thoroughly. Gradually add hot broth to beaten eggs, stirring constantly. Pour over meat balls and cook uncovered 1 to 2 minutes or only long enough to thicken but not curdle the eggs. Serve meat balls in the sauce. Makes 4 servings.

☙ SOUTH AFRICAN GROUND BEEF PIE (BABOTTEE)

- 2 tablespoons butter or margarine
- 2 onions, chopped
- 1 slice white bread
- ¾ cup milk
- 1 lb. finely ground beef
- 1 egg, beaten
- 2 tablespoons curry powder
- 1½ teaspoons salt
- ¼ cup plum jam
- 2 tablespoons fresh lemon juice
- ¼ cup ground almonds
- 3 bay leaves
- 1 egg

Melt butter or margarine in large skillet or frying pan over moderate heat; add onions; cook about 10 minutes or until lightly browned, stirring frequently. Moisten bread with milk; squeeze dry, reserving the milk; mash bread fine. Mix together ground beef, cooked onions, bread, egg, curry powder, salt, plum jam, lemon juice, and ground almonds. Beat 3 to 4 minutes until light. Place bay leaves on bottom of greased shallow casserole; place meat mixture on top. Mix together remaining egg and reserved milk; pour over meat mixture. Bake in a moderate oven (350°F.) about 1½ hours or until done. Serve hot. Makes 4 servings.

⊰§ VEAL SCALLOPINI

(The day Julius La Rosa visited me in the kitchen)

Cinderella in her full regalia could not have been more excited than I was the day that Julius La Rosa came into my kitchen. I had been told that he might appear and would I please cook something special for him. I didn't have much time to decide what to cook, but one thing I knew for certain: whatever it was, it had to be unique. The dish I chose was Veal Scallopini, made without tomato sauce. Maybe you have eaten it. The thin pounded veal cutlet is floured slightly and then browned in olive oil over fast heat, and then just a bit of garlic and rosemary are added along with white wine, and it's cooked quickly and served with the pan juices. It was so wonderful to see Julius in person. You see, I had watched him since the first day he had been on the Godfrey show, when he came on half scared and didn't know what to do with his hands. Julius was so boyish in those days and so refreshing that a neighbor and I who used to watch television together paid little attention to his singing, we liked him so much as a person. We'd root for him when he'd put a song over. I believe his eagerness to make good was the spirit we caught; in ensuing years as I watched his rise I always gloated with pride, as if he had been my own relative. When this well-groomed very sedate young man walked in toward me I yelled out, "Julius, I know you —you were still a gob when I saw you singing your first song on the Godfrey Show." Bless his heart, he greeted me as if I had been some long-lost cousin: guess I took him by surprise. During our lengthy greeting the pan of meat got so hot that when I added the wine such a gush of steam surrounded us that for a moment we were obscured from sight. After all, what do you expect from a gal when a dream man comes to life in her very own kitchen, but to completely forget her pots and pans? Now, it was some four or five years since I first saw Julius La Rosa make his bow to the public. That he had gained composure and self assurance was to be expected. He was most gracious and appreciative. I said to myself, "No wonder he's been such a big success." If you'll dig a bit, you'll find that many of the big stars are great because they have that quality of humility, which is the secret of greatness.

Here's the recipe:

- 1 lb. veal cutlet pounded thin
- 3 tablespoons flour
- ½ teaspoon salt
- ¼ teaspoon ground black pepper
- 3 tablespoons olive oil
- 1 teaspoon whole rosemary leaves, crumbled
- 1 clove garlic, minced
- 1½ cups white wine
- Salt and ground black pepper
- 1 lemon, sliced

Cut meat into portion-sized pieces. Coat with mixture of flour, salt, and pepper. Heat oil in large skillet or frying pan. Add veal and brown on both sides over high heat. Reduce heat. Add rosemary, garlic, and wine. Cook 6 to 8 minutes or until slightly thickened pan gravy has formed and meat is done. Season to taste. Serve with pan juices and lemon. Makes 4 servings.

❧ VEAL BASQUE

- 2 lbs. stewing veal, cut into pieces
- 1 teaspoon salt
- ¼ teaspoon ground black pepper
- ¼ lb. butter or margarine
- 6 to 8 medium mushroom caps, quartered
- ½ small egg plant, peeled and cut into finger-like strips
- 1 green pepper, cut into ½″ strips
- 3 tomatoes, peeled and quartered
- 9 small onions, boiled 10 minutes and drained
- 1 clove garlic, minced
- 1 to 2 bay leaves
- ½ teaspoon whole thyme leaves, crumbled
- ¼ teaspoon ground black pepper
- 1½ teaspoons salt
- ¾ cup dry white wine

Sprinkle veal with salt and pepper. Heat butter in large skillet or frying pan over moderate heat until frothy; add veal; cook until browned, stirring often. Lift out veal pieces and place in greased shallow casserole. Place vegetables in fat in skillet; add garlic, bay leaves, thyme, pepper, salt, and wine; cook 6 to 7 minutes, stirring frequently. Arrange vegetables and juices over veal. Cover and bake in a moderate oven (350°F.) about 45 to 50 minutes or until done. Serve from casserole. Makes 4 to 6 servings.

❧ COLD PRESSED VEAL AND CHICKEN

- 2½ lbs. veal shank or neck
- 1 small onion, sliced
- 1 celery stalk and leaves, cut up
- 6 cups boiling water
- 2 teaspoons salt
- 6 to 8 peppercorns
- 1 tablespoon mixed pickling spices
- 1 lb. chicken necks from broiler-fryers
- 1 small onion
- 1 stalk celery
- 1 envelope plain unflavored gelatine
- ¼ cup cold water
- 1 cup cider vinegar
- 2 hard-cooked eggs, sliced
- 1 tablespoon chopped parsley
- Sliced stuffed olives for garnish

Place together veal, onion, celery, boiling water, salt, peppercorns, and pickling spices in Dutch oven or kettle over moderate heat. Cover and simmer 1 hour. Add chicken necks. Cover and simmer 50 minutes to 1 hour or until veal and chicken are cooked enough to leave the bones. Strain and measure broth; add water if needed to make 2½ cups; set aside. Carefully pick meat off veal and chicken bones. Coarsely grind together veal, chicken, onion, and celery. Soften gelatine in water in cup; stand cup in hot water until gelatine is dissolved; add to hot broth with vinegar, stirring until blended. Cool and chill until broth begins to thicken to consistency of unbeaten egg white. Add meat, eggs, and parsley, mixing together until blended. Turn into greased 10 x 5 x 3-inch loaf pan; chill 10 to 12 hours or overnight until firm enough to slice. Unmold on chilled platter. Garnish top with sliced stuffed olives. Slice across for serving. Serve as a main dish for summer meal or buffet. Makes 8 servings.

MEDALLIONS OF VEAL

- 1 lb. veal cutlet ¼ inch thick
- 2 teaspoons salt
- 2 tablespoons butter or margarine (for meat)
- 2 tablespoons butter or margarine (for sauce)
- 4 tablespoons flour
- ⅛ teaspoon ground black pepper
- ⅛ teaspoon ground nutmeg
- 1 cup milk
- ¼ cup grated Swiss cheese
- ¼ cup finely chopped cooked mushrooms
- Crisp parsley, sliced tomatoes, and cucumbers for garnish

Cut veal into 2-inch ovals or rounds; sprinkle with salt. Use trimmings in meat loaf or patties. Heat butter in skillet or frying pan over moderate heat until frothy. Add meat. Cook 5 minutes on each side, or until lightly browned;

place on heat-proof serving platter or plates. Meanwhile, heat remaining butter in small saucepan over low heat until frothy; add flour, stirring constantly; add pepper and nutmeg. Gradually add milk, still stirring constantly. Cook until thickened and smooth; remove from heat; add cheese and mushrooms; blend. Spread sauce evenly over meat medallions. Broil 3 inches from heat in pre-heated broiler about 5 minutes or until puffed and golden. Garnish with parsley, sliced tomatoes, and cucumbers. Makes 4 servings.

◆§ VEAL STEW WITH PRUNES

Everyone knows that veal is rather a bland meat and is always better if it is pepped up with fruit or something with a pungent and decided flavor. This veal stew with prunes is popular. You'll find this boneless cut-up veal in your supermarket.

¼ cup flour
½ teaspoon salt
¼ teaspoon ground black pepper
2 lbs. boneless veal, cut into 1½ inch cubes
3 tablespoons butter or margarine
1 cup water
12 uncooked dried prunes
1 tablespoon cider vinegar
1 tablespoon sugar
¾ cup fresh orange juice
1/16 teaspoon ground cloves
¾ to 1 teaspoon salt
Hot buttered noodles

Mix together flour, salt, and pepper; roll meat in mixture, coating evenly. Heat butter in saucepan; add meat; cook until evenly browned, turning frequently. Add water; cover and simmer about 1 hour or until half-cooked. Add prunes, vinegar, sugar, orange juice, cloves, and salt. Cover and simmer over low heat about 1 hour longer, or until meat is tender. Add a small amount of water if necessary during cooking. Serve over hot buttered noodles. Makes 4 to 6 servings.

☙ WIENER SCHNITZEL AND PLUM DUMPLINGS
(The day Joseph Schildkraut was our guest)

The director of the show briefed me ahead of time that Joseph Schildkraut would be a guest on the show and would I please make something he liked. It wasn't hard to find out that Joseph Schildkraut is a connoisseur of good food. Also, I knew a family who had known his family and I learned that he liked Wiener Schnitzel and Plum Dumplings. Fresh plums were in season so it was no problem to find the makings for them. The meat for Wiener Schnitzel, veal, is always available, and you can buy the thin slices of veal already flattened out for it in your supermarket, or from your local butcher. Let me warn you though, after you bring it home it will need more flattening. It's flat all right, as sold, but for good Wiener Schnitzel and authentic Wiener Schnitzel, the meat should be pounded as thin as wrapping paper. You do this by putting the meat between two sheets of wax paper and then pounding; for want of a better weapon, use a rolling pin, or the edge of a heavy plate. Take great care that you don't break through the paper, and pound evenly so that you get an even thinness. Then the veal is dipped in flour, then in beaten egg, and finally in fine bread crumbs. Then it's cooked very quickly, almost searing it, in butter in a skillet over high heat. And the authentic Wiener Schnitzel I'm told is served with just a piece of lemon. Since we knew Joseph Schildkraut was interested in food we sent him some schnitzel and a plum dumpling, which he nibbled as he chatted with Jinx. He was in ecstasy over both. In fact, after the show was over great Joseph Schildkraut came behind the scene, complimented me, and chatted with me a bit. He told me how this brought back memories of his childhood. It made me feel so good! You know how you feel when you extend yourself to prepare something special for your husband and family and they pat you on the back and say, "Mom, you're wonderful—umm, that was so good." I guess that's something akin to what I felt that day. You might like to try your hand at making the plum dumplings. They're very simple to do. Just get fresh blue freestone plums and pit them. Each one makes a dumpling. Put a little piece of cube sugar and a little piece of lemon peel inside each pitted plum, and wrap it in a thin square (1/8 inch thick)—a square, that is, of biscuit dough. Roll them up as you would an apple dumpling. Then poach them in slightly salted water for about 15 minutes. Serve them with melted butter and sugar. They're delicious, and real old-world. Two or three make one serving. As far as recipes go, both of these dishes merit an award, but I think that Joseph Schildkraut merits the gold skillet award for being such a fine gracious gentleman.

ROAST LEG OF LAMB

1 4 to 6 lb. leg of lamb
1 clove garlic, sliced
1 tablespoon mint flakes
1 to 1½ teaspoons salt
¼ teaspoon ground black pepper
2 cups commercial sour cream
1 cup hot water
2 tablespoons flour
½ cup cold water
Salt and ground black pepper, to taste

Remove the fell or thin paper-like covering on lamb (this makes for easier carving). Make small gashes in surface of meat; tuck garlic slices down into gashes. Rub entire outside with mint flakes, salt, and pepper. Place meat on platter. Coat completely with sour cream. Place uncovered in refrigerator about 4 to 6 hours or until the sour cream has formed a dry crust. Place meat, fat-side-up, on rack in shallow pan. Roast uncovered in a slow oven (325°F.) about 2 hours. Remove roast from oven; crack surface with knife, so that crust falls into pan, forming basis of gravy. Return to oven; continue baking about ½ to 1 hour longer or until done as you desire. Allow 30 minutes per pound for medium done; 35 to 38 minutes per pound for well done. Lift roast onto serving platter and keep warm. For gravy, pour hot water into roasting pan; place over moderate heat. Stir flour and water together until smooth. Gradually add to boiling liquid in roasting pan, stirring constantly until thickened and smooth. Add salt and pepper to taste. Serve sliced lamb with gravy on the side. Makes 8 to 12 servings.

NOTE: Serve with mint jelly and baked sweet potatoes.

◆§ SCANDINAVIAN LAMB AND CABBAGE (FAARKAL)

- 2 lbs. lamb shoulder, cut into 1½-inch chunks
- 3 tablespoons butter or margarine
- Flour
- 1 large head cabbage, cut into 16 wedges
- 1½ teaspoons salt
- 1 teaspoon peppercorns
- 1½ cups boiling water
- Hot boiled potatoes

Select fattiest pieces of meat; place fat-side down in Dutch oven or kettle over moderate heat. Add butter. Coat remaining meat with flour. Arrange a layer of cabbage wedges over meat. Sprinkle with salt. Cover with alternate layers of lamb and cabbage, sprinkling a little of the salt on each layer. Tie peppercorns in small spice bag and add. Add boiling water. Cover and simmer about 1½ to 2 hours, or until meat is tender. Remove peppercorns; serve meat and cabbage with hot boiled potatoes. Makes 6 servings.

CRUSTY PAN-FRIED LIVER FINGERS

1 lb. beef, lamb, or calf liver, sliced ¾ inch thick
⅓ cup flour
¾ teaspoon salt
¾ teaspoon paprika
¼ teaspoon ground black pepper
⅓ cup butter or margarine
1 tablespoon wine vinegar or fresh lemon juice
2 to 3 tablespoons white wine
2 tablespoons chopped parsley

Pull off outer membrane and cut away any tubes from liver; cut into finger-sized strips. Mix together flour, salt, paprika, and pepper; place in small paper bag. Add liver; grasp top of bag shut; shake vigorously 1 to 2 minutes or until liver is evenly floured. Spread liver out on dry surface; let stand about 30 minutes or until partially dried. Heat butter in large skillet or frying pan over high heat until frothy. Add liver, spreading out over entire pan. Cook 4 to 5 minutes or until browned and done, shaking pan and turning the liver fingers over repeatedly. Lift onto warm serving platter. Add vinegar and wine to pan juices; cook 1½ to 2 minutes or until a rich sauce forms, stirring constantly. Pour over liver; sprinkle parsley on top. Serve at once. Makes 4 servings.

SAUSAGE AND LIVER ROLLS IN TOMATO SAUCE

1¼ to 1½ lbs. calf or beef liver, thinly sliced
1 teaspoon salt
½ teaspoon ground black pepper
⅛ teaspoon ground thyme leaves
⅛ teaspoon ground marjoram leaves
6 large pork sausage links
2 tablespoons salad oil
1 can (8 or 9 oz.) tomato sauce

Cut liver into 6 servings; sprinkle with salt, pepper, thyme, and marjoram. Roll each slice around one sausage link; fasten with toothpicks. Heat oil in large skillet or frying pan. Add liver rolls and brown evenly, turning often. Pour off fat. Add tomato sauce. Cover and simmer about 30 to 45 minutes, or until tender. Makes 6 servings.

❧ TRIPE CREOLE

1 lb. fresh honeycomb tripe partly cooked, as bought
Boiling water
1 tablespoon white vinegar
1 tablespoon salt
3 tablespoons butter or margarine
1 large onion, sliced
1 clove garlic, minced
1 green pepper, diced
2 cups canned tomatoes
½ teaspoon ground thyme leaves
1 teaspoon salt
¼ teaspoon ground black pepper
Hot cooked rice

Wash and drain tripe. Cover with boiling water in saucepan; add vinegar and salt. Cover and simmer about 2½ to 2¾ hours, or until tender but slightly chewy. Drain; cut tripe into 1 x 2-inch strips. Set aside. Heat butter or margarine in saucepan over moderate heat until frothy; add onion, garlic, and green pepper; cook uncovered 10 to 15 minutes, or until soft, stirring frequently. Add tomatoes, thyme, salt, and pepper. Cover and simmer 45 minutes. Add tripe; cover and simmer ½ hour longer, or until tender. Serve with hot cooked rice. Makes 4 servings.

7. *Eggs and Cheese*

ABOUT EGGS

Eggs should always be refrigerated, but egg whites, after separating, should be allowed to stand and come to room temperature before whipping, to give more volume.

Hard-cooked eggs for deviling, etc., need careful timing in the cooking so as to have a nice golden yellow yolk and no hint of green. Here's how:

Have eggs at room temperature. Check eggs to be cooked and make sure they have no cracks in the shell. Use a large enough saucepan so that 1 dozen eggs will be in at least 2 quarts of water.

Fill saucepan half-full of water. Lower eggs into water; this breaks the fall of the egg onto the bottom of the pot and prevents cracks. Cover the eggs at least 2 inches above the tops with water.

Place over high heat and quickly bring to a boil; remove from heat. Count time or use timer. Cover; let stand 14 to

15 minutes; no longer. Small eggs need only 12 minutes. Pour off boiling water at once; cool immediately with cold water. To peel off shell, tap the egg gently on a hard surface, cracking the shell all around. Dip into cold water; begin at the large end where air space is and peel off shell, dipping egg repeatedly into cold water. Eggs that are too fresh won't give up their shells without tearing the egg white, no matter how much care one takes.

I've had trouble peeling some eggs that were not fresh, no matter how careful I was. The experts couldn't tell me why. My conclusion? Just one of those things!

Any experienced cook will have no trouble separating egg whites and yolks. Here's what to do if such is not your skill:

Stand a small funnel upright in a cup or small container. Break one egg at a time into the funnel. Lift the funnel and hold until all the egg white has drained into cup. The unbroken egg yolk remains in the funnel.

◆ EGGS IN ASPIC

2 envelopes plain unflavored gelatine
2 cans (10½ oz. each) consomme
¼ teaspoon onion salt
2 teaspoons fresh lemon juice
½ cup pimiento strips
½ cup thinly sliced celery
6 hard-cooked eggs
Crisp salad greens
Curry mayonnaise (see below)

Sprinkle gelatine in ½ cup cold consomme; heat remaining consomme to boiling. Add softened gelatine to hot consomme; stir until gelatine is dissolved. Add onion salt and lemon juice; cool. Arrange pimiento strips in bottom of 2-quart ring mold; gently spoon enough cooled consomme mixture over pimiento to barely cover. Chill until firm;

meanwhile chill consomme mixture until slightly thickened. Fold celery and remaining pimiento into thickened consomme. Arrange eggs equidistant over pimiento strips in mold; pour on thickened gelatine mixture. Chill until firm; unmold on crisp salad greens and serve with curry mayonnaise. Makes 6 servings.

Curry Mayonnaise

Add 1 teaspoon curry powder to 1 tablespoon mayonnaise; mix smooth. Stir into 1 cup mayonnaise.

☙ EGG FOO YUNG

- 6 slices bacon, chopped fine
- 1 large onion, sliced
- 1 cup sliced celery
- 6 eggs
- 1 teaspoon salt
- 1 cup canned bean sprouts, drained
- 1 tablespoon chopped parsley
- 1 cup chopped cooked ham
- 4 scallions, sliced
- 3 tablespoons bouillon
- 4 to 6 tablespoons peanut oil

Cook bacon in large skillet or frying pan until crisp. Add onion; cook 2 minutes, stirring constantly. Remove from heat. Drain off excess fat; add celery; cool. Beat together eggs and salt only enough to blend whites and yolks evenly. Add cooked bacon mixture, bean sprouts, parsley, ham, scallions, and bouillon; stir well. Heat oil in large skillet or frying pan until hot but not smoking. Drop in big spoonfuls of egg and vegetable mixture to make cakes about 3 inches across. Shape cakes round before the egg sets. Cook until set and lightly browned. Turn and brown on underside. Lift onto absobent paper, then onto heated platter. Serve piping hot, plain or with sauce. Makes 6 servings.

Sauce for Egg Foo Yung

1 tablespoon cornstarch
¾ cup bouillon
2 teaspoons soy sauce

Mix together cornstarch, bouillon, and soy sauce in small saucepan. Bring to a boil and cook until clear, stirring constantly. Pour over Egg Foo Yung.

◆§ OLD FASHIONED PICKLED EGGS

(Must be made 2 to 3 days before serving)

2 tablespoons brown sugar
1 teaspoon salt
5 to 6 peppercorns
2 to 3 whole cloves
¼ teaspoon whole dill seed
¼ teaspoon whole celery seed
1 bay leaf
Small piece whole ginger
1 cup cider vinegar
1 cup finely chopped pickled beets
1½ cups pickled beet juice
½ small onion, chopped
12 hard-cooked eggs, shelled

Mix together sugar, salt, spices, vinegar, beets, beet juice, and onion in saucepan. Cook over moderate heat until mixture comes to a boil. Lower heat and simmer uncovered, 3 to 4 minutes. Remove from heat and cool until warm. Pack eggs in bowl or wide-mouthed jar. Pour warm mixture over eggs, gently pushing top eggs into the liquid. Store tightly covered in refrigerator 2 to 3 days before using. Will keep 2 to 3 weeks in refrigerator. To serve, drain eggs; use in salads or whole for picnics and cook-outs. Makes 12 pickled eggs.

✤ ELEGANT BAKED-STEAMED EGGS ON SPINACH WITH CANADIAN BACON

- 2 tablespoons butter or margarine, at room temperature
- 1 cup chopped cooked fresh spinach, drained
- ¼ cup heavy cream
- 4 eggs
- Salt
- Ground pepper
- 4 to 6 slices broiled Canadian-style bacon

Spread butter evenly inside heavy shallow earthen baking dish; spread spinach in bottom of dish; pour cream on top. One by one, carefully break eggs into cream; season with salt and pepper. Stand baking dish in slightly larger baking pan; place in pre-heated moderate oven (350°F.). Pour boiling water into pan around baking dish up to ½ inch of its brim. Cover and bake 10 to 12 minutes or until egg whites are set but not hard, and yolks glossy. Serve in casserole with Canadian bacon on the side. Makes 4 to 6 servings.

✤ BOLOGNA AND EGG PANCAKE À LA BROADWAY

- 4 to 5 slices (¼ lb.) garlic bologna
- 1 tablespoon butter or margarine
- 4 eggs, slightly beaten
- ½ teaspoon salt
- 4 tablespoons cold water

Remove skin from bologna; cut into fourths. Heat butter in medium skillet over moderate heat until frothy; add bologna; cook until bologna begins to curl but is not brown. Mix together eggs, salt, and water; pour over bologna; lower heat. Cook until eggs have begun to cook firm on the bottom; slip a spatula under the firmed eggs, allowing liquid eggs to flow underneath as eggs set on the bottom.

When mixture is still soft, place under broiler heat 2 to 3 minutes to lightly brown the top. Turn out upside down on heated serving platter. Makes 4 servings.

MATZO BRIE

2 matzos
Warm water
3 eggs, beaten
¼ to ½ teaspoon salt
⅛ teaspoon ground pepper
3 tablespoons salad oil, fat, or margarine
Sugar or applesauce

Break matzos roughly into 1½ inch squares; cover with warm water in bowl and let stand 2 minutes. Drain matzos; press out excess water. Combine beaten eggs, matzos, salt, and pepper. Heat oil in skillet or frying pan until hot but not smoking; add matzos mixture. Cook covered, 10 minutes or until firm. Turn matzo brie over by inverting on plate placed on top; slip back into pan; cook uncovered, 3 to 4 minutes, or until golden brown on underside. Serve with sugar or applesauce. Makes 2 large or 4 small servings.

CHEESE ONION PUFF

4 slices caraway rye bread, cut in half
½ cup chopped onion
8 slices (½ lb.) process American cheese
2 eggs
1 teaspoon salt
⅛ teaspoon garlic salt
½ teaspoon prepared mustard
2½ cups hot milk
2 tablespoons butter or margarine
Paprika

Place one layer of bread on bottom of greased shallow casserole; sprinkle half the onion on top. Cover with one layer of cheese. Repeat with remaining bread, onion, and cheese. Beat eggs with salt, garlic salt, and mustard, until blended. Gradually add hot milk, stirring constantly. Slowly pour over bread-cheese combination. Dot with butter; sprinkle with paprika. Bake uncovered in a moderate oven (350°F.) about 35 to 40 minutes, or until slightly puffed and browned. Serve hot, cut into squares or wedges. Makes 4 servings.

NOTE: Excellent luncheon or supper dish. Perfect for hot buffet.

☙ COTTAGE CHEESE BLINTZES

1 cup sifted all-purpose flour
1 tablespoon sugar
⅛ teaspoon salt
2 eggs, beaten
1½ cups milk
2 tablespoons melted butter or margarine
Oil to grease pan
1½ cups cottage cheese
1 tablespoon sugar
⅛ teaspoon cinnamon
Butter or margarine to pan-fry blintzes
Commercial sour cream

Sift together flour, sugar, and salt into mixing bowl; add eggs and half of the milk, beating until smooth and lump-free. Add remaining milk and butter, beating until a smooth, thin batter forms. Heat small frying pan or skillet over moderate heat. Coat with small amount of oil on soft paper; pour in enough batter to coat bottom of pan; cook until firmed. Flip pan upside down onto a clean towel, tapping pan so pancake or blintze falls out. Repeat, oiling frying pan and making thin pancakes or blintzes, and turning them out on clean towel. Mix together cottage cheese, sugar, and cinnamon. Place spoonful of mixture in center of each blintze; roll up making snug rolls. Place 1 tablespoon butter in large skillet or frying pan over moderate heat; add rolled blintzes; cook until lightly browned and hot, gently turning them over repeatedly for even browning. Serve hot with sour cream spooned on top. Makes 12 blintzes.

WELSH RAREBIT

- 2 tablespoons butter or margarine
- 1 lb. sharp cheddar cheese, shredded
- 2 teaspoons cornstarch
- ⅛ teaspoon dry powdered mustard
- ¼ teaspoon salt
- 2 tablespoons water
- 1 cup ale
- Few drops Tabasco
- 4 to 6 slices hot buttered toast

Heat butter over moderate heat in skillet or frying pan until frothy; or use chafing dish pan directly over heat. Add cheese; stir constantly until cheese has melted. Mix together cornstarch, mustard, salt, and water until smooth; add to melted cheese, stirring rapidly until blended. Gradually add ale and Tabasco, while stirring constantly. Cook 2 to 4 minutes, or until smooth and slightly stringy upon lifting the spoon. Cut toast diagonally across and place in heated shallow casserole; pour bubbling hot rarebit on top. Makes 2 large or 4 small servings.

NOTE: Serving casserole should be hot enough to keep rarebit bubbling.

SPINACH PARMESAN CHEESE SOUFFLE

- 4 egg yolks
- 3 tablespoons butter or margarine
- 3 tablespoons flour
- 1 cup hot milk
- ⅛ teaspoon ground nutmeg
- ¼ teaspoon garlic powder
- ¾ teaspoon salt
- ⅛ teaspoon ground black pepper
- ½ cup grated Parmesan cheese
- 1 cup chopped cooked fresh spinach, drained
- 4 egg whites

Beat egg yolks until thick and lemon colored; set aside. Heat butter in saucepan over moderate heat until frothy and beginning to brown; add flour, stirring rapidly. Gradually add milk, stirring constantly until thickened and smooth. Add nutmeg, garlic powder, salt, and pepper; remove from heat. Add about 1/3 of hot mixture to egg yolks, stirring constantly. Stir back into remaining hot mixture. Add cheese and spinach; mix thoroughly. Beat egg whites until soft mounds form. Add about 2/3 of beaten egg whites to spinach mixture, mixing thoroughly. Gently fold in remaining egg whites. Grease bottom of 1½-quart casserole; pour in mixture. Bake uncovered in pre-heated moderate oven (375°F.) about 30 minutes or until puffed and lightly browned on top. Serve at once. Makes 6 servings.

☙ DUTCH EGG AND HAMBURG NESTS

1 tablespoon butter or margarine
1 chopped onion
1 lb. ground chuck
2 cups soft bread crumbs
1 chopped hard-cooked egg
½ teaspoon curry powder
½ teaspoon salt
½ cup fine dry bread crumbs
Butter or margarine
4 eggs
Crisp lettuce
Sweet gherkins

Melt butter in skillet or frying pan over moderate heat; add onion; cook until clear; remove from heat. Add beef, bread crumbs, chopped egg, curry powder, and salt; blend. Shape into 4 large doughnut-shaped rings; coat with fine bread crumbs; chill 1 hour or longer. To serve, melt 2 to 4 tablespoons butter in large skillet or frying pan over moderate heat; add beef rings; cook 4 to 5 minutes on one side. Turn over carefully and cook 5 to 6 minutes or until done. Break 1 egg into each ring; lower heat. Cover and cook 3 to 4 minutes or until eggs are done. Lift carefully onto lettuce leaves; garnish with gherkins. Wonderful for brunch or lunch. Makes 4 servings.

CASSEROLE OF TOMATOES AND EGGS AU GRATIN

- 3 tablespoons butter or margarine
- 3 tablespoons flour
- 1½ cups milk
- ½ cup grated Parmesan cheese
- 1½ teaspoons salt
- 6 hard-cooked eggs
- 3 large ripe tomatoes
- 1 cup soft bread crumbs
- 2 tablespoons melted butter or margarine

Heat butter in saucepan over moderate heat; stir in flour; gradually add milk. Cook until thickened and smooth, stirring constantly. Add cheese and salt. Blend; remove from heat. Cut eggs in half; place around inside rim of shallow 1½-quart baking dish. Place sliced tomatoes in center. Pour sauce over tomatoes and eggs. Mix together bread crumbs and butter; spread on top. Bake in a moderate oven (350°F.) about 25 to 30 minutes or until bubbly and golden brown on top. Makes 6 servings.

SAN FRANCISCO LITTLE SHRIMP OMELETES

- 6 eggs
- 2 cups sliced celery
- 1 lb. cooked cleaned shrimp (1⅓ cups)
- ¾ teaspoon salt
- ⅛ teaspoon ground pepper
- ½ to ¾ cup oil
- 2 cups hot cooked rice
- Soy sauce

Break eggs into mixing bowl; beat until blended but not frothy. Add celery, shrimp, salt, and pepper; blend. Heat oil in large skillet or frying pan (oil should be ¼ inch deep) over high heat until very hot but not smoking. Drop large spoonfuls of shrimp mixture side by side into hot oil. Gently press outer edges of each little omelet toward its center with spoon. When barely firmed, turn and cook about 2 minutes or until lightly browned and done. Lift out with pancake turner and serve on bed of hot cooked rice. Pass soy sauce. Makes 4 to 6 servings.

8. Salads

Salads have an important and special place of their own in our American menu, both at home and in public eating places. There are four major types of salads:

a) The *appetizer* or the small serving—usually an hors d'oeuvres type of salad to stimulate the appetite.

b) The *main-meal* salad—a hearty well-balanced salad.

c) The *accompaniment* salad—the most common type in the salad family. It is generally served as part of the main course of the meal and is usually comprised of salad greens or a combination of salad greens and vegetables or fruits, served with a zesty French dressing.

d) The *dessert* salad—usually a sweet salad, generally composed of fruits, fresh, canned, or frozen, and often served in a molded form, made with a fruit-flavored gelatine. Sweet or tart French dressing goes well with the dessert salad.

The "salad bowl tossed salad," composed mostly of crisp salad greens, seasoned with your choice of herbs and the kind of dressing, sweet or tart, which your family likes best, is probably America's top favorite. You will find salad greens, in one form or another, all year 'round at your green grocer's or produce department of your food store. Here is a list of the most common varieties: Iceberg Lettuce, Boston Lettuce, Leaf Lettuce, Bibb Lettuce, Romaine, Chicory, Belgian Endive, Escarole, Watercress, Parsley, Celery Tops, Beet Greens, Mustard Greens, Green and Red Cabbage, and several others.

The salad greens are noted for their rich supply of vitamins and minerals needed by the body every day, and each ingredient with its own characteristic flavor offers a variety of choices for your "salad of the day."

VEGETABLE SALADS

Vegetable salads have become quite popular of late years. They are usually composed of cooked vegetables and combine well with cooked meats, fish, and cheese. From the standpoint of popularity, potato salad no doubt leads the parade of the vegetable salads. Bean salads and macaroni salads too, all of which can be included in the so-called "main dish salads," are easy to make and are filling. These can be served hot or cold, and their flavors can vary according to this or that herb or salad dressing you wish to use.

Tomatoes are one of the most flavorful, nutritious, colorful, and adaptable ingredients within the realm of salad making. They can be sliced and served on top of crisp lettuce leaves, with a zippy French-type dressing and a few sprigs of crispy watercress for color contrast and flavor . . . all made in a very few minutes. This is a popular salad and so easy to make. But it can be served in other attractive ways. A favorite partner is cream cheese, served on top or on the side of a tomato slice and garnished with thinly sliced rings of red or green sweet pepper, perkily placed on crisp salad greens. Or a tomato, resting in a cup made of crisp lettuce leaves, stuffed with chicken or macaroni salad, makes an attractive combination and good eating. The tomato lends itself to many combinations and can be cut and arranged in various patterns to suit the creative homemaker.

FRUIT SALADS

Another popular salad, which may precede the meal or be an accompaniment to the meal, or even be the main dish of the meal, is the beloved fruit salad. This is the most colorful of all salads. It can be made from fresh fruit or canned fruit or frozen fruit. It particularly lends itself to luncheon plates as an appetizer, as an accompaniment, or as a delicious dessert salad. Molded gelatine salads are included in this group; it is advisable to follow directions as given on the gelatine package. There are so many fruits from which to select that a home-maker with a creative instinct can allow her imagination to run far afield and find that she has made a new wonderful salad creation.

SALAD DRESSINGS

No matter how good, how perfect, and with how much loving care the ingredients in your salad have been selected, prepared, and arranged, the salad dressing is the final ingredient which determines the success of your efforts. It should be a perfect partner to your salad in flavor and consistency. Make the dressings yourself. They are easy to make and always handy on your refrigerator shelf for a quick meal or unexpected guest. Here are a few basic salad dressings, which can be easily varied to suit the tastes of the family by adding a little of "this or that."

BOILED DRESSING

½ teaspoon salt
1 teaspoon powdered dry mustard
2 tablespoons sugar
Few grains cayenne
3 tablespoons flour
2 egg yolks
1 cup milk
⅓ cup cider vinegar
2 tablespoons butter or margarine

Place salt, mustard, sugar, cayenne, and flour together into top of double boiler. Mix well. Add egg yolks and milk, stirring until smooth. Gradually stir in vinegar. Place over hot, not boiling, water; cook, stirring constantly until thickened and smooth; add butter, stirring until melted; remove from heat. Cool and store, covered, in refrigerator. Thin to desired consistency with milk, cream, or sour cream for use with shredded cabbage for slaw or other vegetables. Makes 1 cup.

BASIC FRENCH DRESSING

1 teaspoon salt
¼ teaspoon celery salt
⅛ teaspoon ground black pepper
¼ teaspoon paprika
1 small clove garlic
¼ cup tarragon wine, cider vinegar, or fresh lemon juice
¾ cup olive or salad oil
1 tablespoon minced parsley

Place salt, celery salt, pepper, paprika, and garlic into mortar or small bowl; mash and stir until garlic is liquefied. Add vinegar; stir until blended. Slowly add oil while stirring rapidly. Add parsley; mix well; cool, but do not chill.

Use on crisp raw greens or vegetables, meat, or fish salads. Makes 1 cup.

MELLOW FRENCH DRESSING

½ teaspoon salt
Few grains of ground black pepper
1 small clove garlic
1 to 2 tablespoons any wine vinegar
1 tablespoon lemon or lime juice
⅔ cup olive or salad oil
1 egg white
¼ cup finely chopped parsley

Place salt and pepper into small jar. Bruise garlic by mashing slightly between fold of small piece aluminum foil. Add garlic, vinegar, lemon juice, oil, egg white, and parsley over seasonings. Cover jar tightly. Shake vigorously for 2 minutes or until slightly thickened. Serve with raw or cooked vegetable, meat, or fish salads. Makes 1 cup.

LOW CALORIE FRENCH DRESSING

1 tablespoon cornstarch
½ teaspoon salt
½ teaspoon celery salt
¼ teaspoon onion salt
1 teaspoon sugar
1 cup water
2 tablespoons salad oil
1 clove garlic
¼ cup vinegar or fresh lemon juice
2 tablespoons ketchup

Place cornstarch, all salts, and sugar together into small saucepan over moderate heat; gradually add water, stirring constantly. Cook 5 to 6 minutes or until slightly thickened and clear, stirring constantly. Remove from heat. Add oil; mix well. Cool. Add garlic, vinegar, and ketchup; beat until smooth. Pour into jar or container; cover. Store in refrigerator. Shake before using. Serve with raw or cooked vegetable, meat, fish or fruit salads. Makes 1 cup.

MAYONNAISE MADE IN ELECTRIC BLENDER

- 1 egg
- 1 teaspoon salt
- 1 teaspoon powdered dry mustard
- ⅛ teaspoon ground white pepper
- 1 tablespoon fresh lemon juice
- 1 cup salad oil

Place egg, salt, mustard, pepper, lemon juice, and ¼ cup oil in blender; blend 20 seconds on medium or high speed; stop blender; add ½ of remaining oil; blend until thick, about 25 seconds; stop blender; add remaining oil; blend until thick, about 25 seconds. Makes about 1½ cups.

BUTTERY GOURMET ROQUEFORT OR BLEU CHEESE DRESSING

- ¼ lb. Roquefort or Bleu cheese, at room temperature
- ¼ lb. soft butter or margarine
- ½ teaspoon garlic salt
- 2 teaspoons vinegar
- 2 teaspoons Worcestershire sauce
- Few drops Tabasco sauce

Mash cheese until creamy; add butter; mash; then beat 4 to 5 minutes or until fluffy. Add garlic salt, vinegar, Worcestershire and Tabasco sauce; mix thoroughly. Store at room temperature. Serve with hearts of lettuce, endive, or romaine. Makes 1¼ cups.

ANCHOVY CARAWAY PARMESAN DRESSING

- ½ teaspoon salt
- ¼ teaspoon garlic salt
- ¼ teaspoon paprika
- ¼ teaspoon ground black pepper
- ½ teaspoon ground caraway seed
- 3 tablespoons wine vinegar
- ¾ cup olive oil
- 1 egg white
- ¼ cup diced anchovy fillets
- 2 tablespoons grated Parmesan cheese

Place salt, garlic salt, paprika, pepper, caraway seed, vinegar, oil, and egg white together into jar. Cover and shake vigorously for 2 minutes or until thickened. Add anchovies and cheese. Mix well. Serve with mixed greens, tossed salad, or chef's salad bowl. Makes about 1½ cups.

☙ COOKED SALAD DRESSING FOR FRUIT

3 tablespoons cornstarch
¼ cup sugar
½ teaspoon salt
¼ teaspoon celery salt
½ cup commercial sour cream
1 cup pineapple juice
1 egg, beaten
¼ cup fresh lemon juice
¼ cup cider vinegar
½ cup heavy cream

Mix together cornstarch, sugar, salt, celery salt, and sour cream in top of double boiler; gradually add pineapple juice, stirring rapidly. Cook over gently boiling water until thick and smooth, stirring constantly. Mix together egg, lemon juice, and vinegar; gradually add to hot mixture, stirring rapidly. Cook 2 to 3 minutes or until egg has cooked. Cool. Cover closely to prevent skin from forming on top. Whip cream and fold in. Makes approximately 2½ cups.

☙ ANTIPASTO POTATO SALAD

2 anchovy fillets
1 clove garlic
¼ cup chopped parsley
1 onion, finely chopped
2 whole stalks celery, chopped fine
½ teaspoon crushed red pepper
½ teaspoon salt
⅓ cup olive oil
⅓ cup red wine vinegar
1 quart diced cooked potatoes
1 tablespoon capers

Mash anchovy fillets and garlic in mixing bowl until smooth. Add parsley, onion, celery, red pepper and salt; blend. Gradually add oil and vinegar. Add potatoes; blend. Chill several hours or overnight. Serve sprinkled with capers as one item of antipasto. Makes 1 quart.

☙ COLD MARINATED CUCUMBERS

2 medium cucumbers
1 cup water
1 teaspoon salt
1 clove garlic, crushed
2 tablespoons fresh lemon juice
3 tablespoons salad oil
¼ cup chopped onion
⅛ teaspoon ground black pepper
2 tablespoons minced parsley

Lightly pare cucumbers; cut lengthwise into sixths; place in skillet or frying pan. Add water, salt and garlic. Cover and simmer for 10 minutes or until tender. Drain; place in shallow dish. Mix together lemon juice, oil, onion and pepper; pour over cucumbers. Sprinkle parsley on top. Chill 2 hours or longer. Serve with cold meat, fish or poultry, or as an appetizer. Makes 4 servings.

☙ ITALIAN MEAT SALAD

2 cups diced cold cooked beef, lamb or veal
1 cup sliced or diced celery
2 tablespoons grated onion
3 tablespoons olive oil
1 tablespoon red wine vinegar
1 tablespoon fresh lemon juice
1 teaspoon salt
⅛ teaspoon ground black pepper
2 tablespoons chopped parsley
Crisp lettuce
Sliced tomatoes for garnish

Combine all ingredients, except lettuce and tomatoes. Chill 2 hours or longer. Serve on crisp lettuce, and garnish with sliced tomatoes. Makes 4 to 6 servings.

☙ MOLDED TUNA FISH AND EGG SALAD

2 cans (7 oz. each) chunk-style tuna
1 tablespoon plain, unflavored gelatine
¼ cup cold water
½ cup boiling water
½ cup mayonnaise or salad dressing
¼ cup ketchup
2 tablespoons fresh lemon juice
½ cup chopped celery
2 tablespoons chopped sweet pickle
2 tablespoons chopped stuffed olives
¼ teaspoon salt
4 to 6 hard-cooked eggs
Crisp salad greens
Mayonnaise or salad dressing

Drain tuna. Soften gelatine in cold water. Add boiling water; stir until dissolved. Cool. Mix together mayonnaise, ketchup and lemon juice. Add gelatine; blend. Fold in celery, pickle, olives and salt. Fold in tuna. Spread one half of mixture in loaf pan. Place eggs end to end on top of mixture. Cover with remaining tuna mixture, pressing down firmly and evenly. Chill 4 hours or longer until firm enough to slice. Unmold on salad greens. Slice and serve with mayonnaise. Makes 6 to 8 servings.

STUFFED ROMAINE

1 package (3-oz.) cream cheese
1 cup cottage cheese
¼ cup chopped green pepper
¼ cup minced onion
¼ cup chopped, drained pimiento
¼ cup chopped parsley
¼ cup sour pickle relish
1 teaspoon salt
⅛ teaspoon ground black pepper
1 medium head Romaine lettuce, crisped
French dressing

Mix together cream cheese and cottage cheese until blended. Add green pepper, onion, pimiento, parsley, relish, salt and pepper. Mix until blended. Separate Romaine leaves. Spread mixture evenly over insides of leaves. Fit leaves together, cheese side turned inward to re-shape compact head. Roll tightly in waxed paper or foil. Refrigerate 3 to 4 hours or longer or until cheese mixture has firmed enough to slice. To serve, slice across into ½-inch thick slices. Serve with French dressing. Makes 4 to 6 servings.

NOTE: To slice, use saw motion with keen-edged knife.

SPICED PEACH AND COTTAGE CHEESE SALAD

1½ cups cottage cheese
2 tablespoons chopped pimiento
½ teaspoon celery salt
6 canned spiced peach halves, chilled (see note)
Crisp salad greens
Mayonnaise
¼ cup chopped nuts

Mix together cheese, pimiento and celery salt. Arrange peaches cut-side up on salad greens. Spoon cheese mixture onto peaches. Garnish with mayonnaise and nuts. Makes 6 servings.

NOTE: Spiced peaches can be made from canned cling peaches. Drain one can cling peaches; add small piece whole cinnamon, 1/4 teaspoon each ground cloves and mace to liquid; heat and pour over peaches. Let stand several hours or longer.

BAKED BEET SALAD

- 6 medium fresh beets
- 1/3 cup French dressing
- 1/2 teaspoon salt
- 1/8 teaspoon ground black pepper
- 1 medium onion, sliced
- Crisp salad greens
- 1 hard-cooked egg, chopped
- Additional French dressing

Trim beets leaving one inch of stems at the top and root ends; wash. Wrap in aluminum foil; bake in hot oven 425°F. 45 to 50 minutes or until cooked. To test: press wrapped beets; if slightly soft, they're done. Cool, wrapped. Slip skins off beets and slice into bowl. Add dressing, salt, pepper and onion; blend; chill 1 hour. Serve on salad greens garnished with chopped egg. Pass French dressing. Makes 6 servings.

MACARONI AND MEAT SALAD

- 1/2 lb. elbow macaroni
- 2 cups diced cooked chicken, turkey or ham
- 1 cup diced celery
- 2 tablespoons grated onion
- 1 teaspoon salt
- 1/4 teaspoon ground black pepper
- 1/2 cup French dressing
- 1/4 cup mayonnaise
- Crisp lettuce
- 1/2 cup mayonnaise
- 2 pimientos, chopped fine
- 6 stuffed olives, sliced

Cook macaroni in boiling salted water until tender; drain, rinse with cold water and refrigerate. Meanwhile, combine chicken, celery, onion, salt, pepper and French dressing in mixing bowl; blend. Chill 15 to 20 minutes or until serving time. At serving time, add macaroni and 1/4 cup mayonnaise to chicken mixture; blend. Arrange on lettuce-lined platter. Lightly coat surface of salad with remaining mayonnaise. Garnish with pimientos and olives. Serves 6.

☙ TOMATO SOUP SALAD

1½ envelope plain unflavored gelatine
¼ cup cold water
1 cup boiling water
1 can (10½ oz.) tomato soup
½ teaspoon sugar
¼ teaspoon garlic salt
⅛ teaspoon ground black pepper
Crisped salad greens
French dressing

Soften gelatine in cold water in bowl. Add boiling water, stirring until dissolved. Add tomato soup, sugar, garlic salt and pepper; blend. Turn into loaf pan; chill until firm. Unmold and slice or cut into cubes. Serve on salad greens with French dressing. Makes 4 to 6 servings.

☙ TOSSED GREEN SALAD

Approximately ⅓ head iceberg or Boston lettuce
Approximately ⅓ to ¼ head romaine
Approximately ⅓ head escarole
Approximately ¼ bunch watercress
4 to 6 scallions or radishes
Approximately ½ cup Basic French Dressing
Salt and ground black pepper to taste

Wash salad greens separately until thoroughly free of grit, taking care not to bruise leaves. Drain thoroughly. Tear lettuce, romaine, and escarole into bite-sized pieces; wrap separately in cloth or paper towels; refrigerate. Carefully wash and pick over watercress; drain; wrap in cloth or paper towels; refrigerate. Trim scallions, retaining 2 to 3 inches of green tops. Slice or cut into match-like strips; refrigerate, covered. If using radishes, slice, reserving tops if fresh and green; refrigerate, covered. Chill salad bowl. At serving time, arrange prepared greens and scallions or radishes in alternate layers in salad bowl. Do not add watercress or radish tops. Sprinkle dressing over greens; toss lightly; taste. Add salt and pepper, if needed. Place watercress and radish leaves on top. Serve. Makes 6 servings.

◆ CHEF'S SALAD

½ head crisp iceberg lettuce
½ head crisp romaine
4 slices boiled tongue, cut into match-like strips
4 slices American cheese, cut into match-like strips
4 hard-cooked eggs, quartered
2 tomatoes, peeled and cut into sixths
1 recipe Salad Topping (see below)

Tear iceberg lettuce and romaine into bite-sized pieces. Arrange layers of iceberg lettuce, romaine, tongue, cheese, eggs, and tomatoes, in large salad bowl; spread lightly with Chef's Salad Topping. Repeat alternating layers with remaining ingredients. Serve at once or chill until served. Makes 6 servings.

Chef's Salad Topping

- 1 cup mayonnaise or salad dressing
- 2 tablespoons French dressing
- 2 tablespoons chopped pimiento
- 1 tablespoon minced onion
- 1 tablespoon minced chives
- ¼ teaspoon whole basil leaves, crumbled

Mix together all ingredients; chill until needed. Makes 1¼ cups.

COLD SEA FOOD PLATTER WITH CHIVE AND PARSLEY DIP

- 1½ cups mayonnaise or salad dressing
- 2 tablespoons fresh lemon or lime juice
- 1 tablespoon minced chives
- 1 tablespoon minced parsley
- ½ lb. cooked chilled crab meat
- ½ lb. cooked chilled lobster meat, diced
- 1 lb. cooked cleaned shrimp, chilled
- Crisp salad greens
- 1 cup diced celery
- 2 tomatoes, peeled and quartered
- Lime wedges

Mix together mayonnaise, lemon or lime juice, chives, and parsley. Chill. Arrange cold sea foods in individual mounds on platter lined with crisp salad greens. Place mound of celery in the center; garnish with quartered tomatoes and lime wedges. Serve chilled mayonnaise dip in separate bowl. Makes 4 to 6 servings.

CRAB MEAT LOUIS COCKTAIL SALAD

- ½ medium head crisp lettuce, shredded
- 1 to 1½ cups cooked or canned lump crab meat, chilled
- 1 large tomato, peeled and cut into 8 wedges
- 6 to 12 strips pimiento
- 2 hard-cooked eggs, chopped fine
- Louis Sauce

Arrange lettuce on individual plates. Place crab meat in a mound on top of lettuce. Arrange tomato wedges and pimiento strips around and over crab. Sprinkle chopped egg on top; chill until serving time. Serve with Louis Sauce spooned over crab. Makes 4 servings.

Louis Sauce

1 cup mayonnaise or salad dressing
½ cup chili sauce
1 tablespoon grated onion
1 small sweet pickle, minced
1 teaspoon grated horseradish
1 teaspoon fresh lemon juice
¼ teaspoon whole tarragon leaves, crumbled
½ teaspoon salt
⅛ teaspoon ground black pepper

Mix together mayonnaise and chili sauce, stirring until blended and smooth. Add onion, pickle, horseradish, lemon juice, tarragon, salt, and pepper, mixing until barely blended. Chill until serving time. Makes 1½ cups.

POTATO AND CRAB MEAT BUFFET SALAD

3 medium potatoes
1 small onion
½ cup consomme or 1 bouillon cube dissolved in ½ cup boiling water
⅓ cup vinegar
1 teaspoon salt
3 tablespoons olive oil
1 can (6½ oz.) king crab meat, membranes removed
Crisp lettuce greens
Freshly ground black pepper
12 anchovy fillets
Capers
1 pimiento, cut into small diamonds
¼ cup chopped parsley

Cook potatoes in boiling salted water to cover, until tender but not broken; drain, peel, and cool. Slice into bowl, making thin chips. Grate onion or place cut-up onion into blender with consomme and vinegar and blend until onion is pureed. If using grated onion, mix together onion, consomme, and vinegar. Place consomme mixture into small saucepan over high heat; add salt. Bring to boiling temperature. Pour over potatoes in bowl. Add oil and crab meat; toss until blended. Turn into lettuce-lined bowl; sprinkle pepper from mill on top. Arrange anchovies criss-cross on top to make diamond pattern. Dot spaces in diamonds with capers and pimiento. Sprinkle parsley in a border around the rim. Serve at room temperature. May be served on a platter without lettuce, accompanied by a mixed green salad. Makes approximately 4 servings.

GLOBE ARTICHOKE SALAD

4 medium-size fresh artichokes
Boiling water
Salt
1 clove garlic, minced
½ onion, sliced
Mayonnaise or salad dressing
Lettuce

Cut artichoke stems to within ½-inch of base. Remove outside bottom leaves. If tips are thorny, snip off thorns with scissors. Wash well under running water. Place upright, close together in deep saucepan. Sprinkle ½ teaspoon salt over each artichoke. Cover with boiling water 2 to 3 inches deep. Add garlic and onion. Cover. Simmer gently about 45 minutes or until base is tender. Test tenderness of base by pulling out one of the leaves. Lift out; drain upside down. Cool. Cut off all stem. Serve upright in individual salad plates with mayonnaise in a small lettuce cup on the side. Makes 4 servings.

NOTE: To eat, pull leaves out one by one; dip base in mayonnaise; hold the leaf tip while scraping off pulp and mayonnaise with teeth. The remaining base, or heart, is the choicest morsel; after all the leaves are eaten, scoop the hairy "choke" off the heart with knife and fork and discard. Break the tender heart in pieces with a fork, dipping each piece in mayonnaise before eating.

◆§ WATERCRESS SALAD

1 bunch watercress
1 cup fresh rye bread crumbs
3 tablespoons olive oil
1 small clove garlic, minced
1 tablespoon grated horseradish
French dressing

Wash cress and drain thoroughly; chill. Combine rye bread crumbs, oil, and garlic in skillet or frying pan. Cook over moderate heat; brown lightly, stirring constantly; cool. Place watercress in salad bowl or on salad plates. Combine cooled toasted rye bread crumbs and grated horseradish; blend. Sprinkle over watercress. Serve with French dressing. Makes 4 servings.

◆§ ROMAINE AND PARMESAN CHEESE SALAD

1 small or ½ large head romaine
1 slice toast
1 clove garlic
2 eggs
3 tablespoons olive or salad oil
1½ tablespoons fresh lemon juice
Salt and ground black pepper
¼ teaspoon Worcestershire sauce
Grated Parmesan cheese

Wash and drain romaine; refrigerate long enough to crisp leaves. Pat each leaf dry. Rub garlic into both sides of toasted bread; cut into squares; place in bottom of salad bowl. Tear dry crisp romaine leaves roughly into bite-sized pieces; pile into bowl over toast. Boil eggs 2 minutes; open eggs, scoop out and spread over romaine. Add oil, lemon juice, salt, pepper, and Worcestershire sauce; toss; sprinkle grated cheese on top. Makes 6 servings.

☙ TURKEY VEGETABLE SALAD

- 1½ cups finely chopped cooked white and dark turkey meat
- 1 cup cold cooked rice
- ¾ cup diced celery
- ¼ cup minced pimiento
- ¼ cup minced green pepper
- ½ teaspoon salt
- Ground black pepper, to taste
- ¾ to 1 cup mayonnaise or salad dressing
- Crisp salad greens
- Capers
- Black olives

Mix together turkey, rice, celery, pimiento, and green pepper. Toss lightly with fork until well-blended. Add salt and pepper. Blend in mayonnaise. Chill thoroughly. Serve on crisp salad greens; garnish with capers and olives. Makes 4 servings.

☙ CLAM ASPIC SALAD

- 1 envelope plain unflavored gelatine
- ¼ cup cold water
- 1 cup boiling water
- 1 can (7 oz.) minced clams and liquid
- 2 tablespoons Worcestershire sauce
- 2 tablespoons fresh lemon juice
- ⅛ teaspoon ground black pepper
- 2 tablespoons minced parsley
- Crisp salad greens
- Russian dressing

Soften gelatine in cold water; add to boiling water in bowl, stirring until dissolved. Add clams, Worcestershire sauce, lemon juice, pepper, and parsley, stirring until blended. Pour into greased loaf pan; cool and chill until firm enough to cut into cubes, or cube in the pan, or unmold and cube. Serve on salad greens; top with Russian dressing. Makes 4 servings.

◆ OLD-FASHIONED CHICKEN SALAD

3 cups cubed white and dark cooked chicken
2 tablespoons lemon juice
3 tablespoons olive oil
1 teaspoon grated onion
1 teaspoon salt
¼ teaspoon ground black pepper
1½ cups diced celery
¾ cup mayonnaise or salad dressing
Crisp salad greens
Capers
Tomato quarters
Radish roses
Pimiento strips

Place chicken, lemon juice, oil, onion, salt, and pepper into mixing bowl and mix together lightly until well-blended. Cover and refrigerate 1 hour or longer. To serve, add celery and mayonnaise to chicken, stirring and folding together until blended. Turn onto chilled salad plates lined with greens. Garnish with capers and all or several of remaining garnishes. Makes 6 servings.

◆ GREEK BEAN SALAD

½ lb. (1 cup) dry navy or pea beans
2 quarts water
2 teaspoons salt
½ cup sliced scallions, with tops
½ cup sliced radishes
½ cup olive oil
¼ cup fresh lemon juice
¾ to 1 teaspoon salt
¼ teaspoon ground black pepper

Wash and drain beans and place in saucepan. Add water and salt and place over high heat. Boil uncovered 10 minutes. Remove from heat; let stand covered 1 hour. Place beans over moderate heat; simmer 1½ to 1¾ hours or until tender. Drain and cool. Combine drained beans, scallions, radishes, olive oil, and lemon juice in bowl. Mix lightly; add salt and pepper. Serve without salad greens with cold cuts, or for buffets, or as part of antipasto. Makes 4 to 6 servings.

◆§ WALDORF SALAD

2 diced, unpared large red apples
2 tablespoons fresh lemon or lime juice
2 teaspoons sugar
⅛ teaspoon salt
1 cup thinly sliced celery
½ cup commercial sour cream
½ cup mayonnaise or salad dressing
Crisp salad greens
½ cup coarsely chopped walnuts
6 to 8 maraschino cherries
Whipped cream for garnish, optional

Combine apples, lemon juice, sugar, and salt in bowl; fold in celery. Add sour cream to mayonnaise, stirring until blended; add to apple mixture, folding until blended. Refrigerate until serving time. Serve on salad greens; sprinkle nuts on top. Garnish with cherries and whipped cream. Makes 6 servings.

◆§ HEALTH BOWL SALAD SUPREME

2 cups crisped shredded cabbage
1 cup coarsely shredded celery leaves
¼ head escarole, coarsely torn into bite-sized pieces
1 cup shredded carrots
½ green pepper, cut into thin match-like strips
¼ cup sliced radishes
1 tablespoon honey
1 tablespoon fresh lemon juice
2 tablespoons mayonnaise or salad dressing
¾ cup buttermilk
1 teaspoon salt
1 cup whole orange sections

Place together cabbage, celery leaves, escarole, carrots, green pepper, and radishes in chilled salad bowl. Mix together honey, lemon juice, mayonnaise, buttermilk, and salt until blended; pour over greens and mix lightly. Garnish with orange sections on top. Makes 4 to 6 servings.

CUCUMBERS IN SOUR CREAM

1 medium cucumber
2 teaspoons salt
¼ cup vinegar
½ to ¾ cup commercial sour cream
Freshly ground black pepper
Chives, fresh dill or dill seed

Pare cucumber lightly to remove any wax coating, but leaving on plenty of green. Score cucumber lightly with tines of fork drawn full-length all around cucumber. Slice as thin as possible; place in shallow bowl. Sprinkle with the salt and vinegar; place in refrigerator about 1½ to 2 hours. Drain and discard juices from cucumber, pressing gently; place into serving dish. Spread sour cream over cucumber; sprinkle with pepper from mill; fold all together lightly; chill. Generously garnish top with scissor-snipped chives or fresh dill, or dill seed. Serve as buffet relish, or as salad. Makes 4 servings.

HAM AND EGG MOUSSE

1 envelope plain unflavored gelatine
1 tablespoon sugar
¼ cup water
1 teaspoon powdered dry mustard
⅓ cup vinegar
4 hard-cooked eggs, chopped fine
1 cup cooked minced ham
1 cup finely diced celery
2 tablespoons sweet pickle relish
1 tablespoon minced parsley
¼ cup fresh lemon juice
½ cup heavy cream, whipped
Crisp salad greens
Mustard mayonnaise (½ cup mayonnaise and 1 tablespoon prepared mustard blended together)

Mix together gelatine, sugar, water, mustard, and vinegar in top of double boiler; let stand 5 minutes. Place over boiling water; cook 5 to 6 minutes or until gelatine is dissolved, stirring constantly. Remove from heat; cool; chill until beginning to thicken and of egg white consistency. Add eggs, ham, celery, pickle relish, parsley, and lemon juice, folding together until blended. Fold in whipped cream. Turn into 1-quart mold or individual molds; chill until firm. Unmold on salad greens; serve sliced with mustard mayonnaise. Makes 6 servings.

NOTE: For a firmer loaf in very hot weather, use 2 envelopes of gelatine.

INDIAN SALAD WITH DANDELION GREENS

- 1 cup cooked or canned kernel corn
- ½ cup shredded raw beets
- 2 cups shredded cabbage
- ½ medium onion, grated
- 1 teaspoon salt
- ⅛ teaspoon ground black pepper
- ⅓ cup French dressing
- Crisp young dandelion greens
- ½ cup cottage cheese

Mix together corn, beets, cabbage, onion, salt, and pepper in bowl. Add French dressing, tossing until blended. Chill until serving time. To serve, line salad plate or plates with dandelion greens. Pile salad mixture onto greens. Place teaspoonfuls of cheese on top. Makes 4 to 6 servings.

MELANGE SALAD (POTATO AND GREEN BEAN SALAD)

- 2 cups diced cold boiled potatoes
- 2 cups sliced cold cooked green beans
- 2 tablespoons wine vinegar
- 6 tablespoons olive oil
- ½ teaspoon salt
- ⅛ teaspoon ground black pepper
- Crisp salad greens
- 8 fillets of anchovies
- 1 can (7 oz.) chunk-style tuna, drained
- 2 tomatoes, sliced or quartered
- 8 ripe olives
- 2 teaspoons capers
- 2 teaspoons chopped parsley

Combine potatoes and green beans. Combine wine vinegar, olive oil, salt, and pepper; mix well; pour over potatoes and beans. Mix lightly; chill several hours. Line shallow salad bowl with crisp salad greens; mound chilled potatoes and beans in center. Arrange anchovies and tuna on top. Garnish with tomatoes and ripe olives. Sprinkle with capers and parsley. Makes 4 to 6 servings.

⁂ FRANKFURTER SALAD BOWL

Now if you have teen-agers in your family this is a dish I think they'll vote for. You've all seen teen-agers dig into beans and you know how they like hot dogs—why not put them together? By the way, the frankfurters here are eaten without cooking—which reminds us that when we buy frankfurters they're fully cooked. We heat them because our folks like to have them hot. Frankfurters are a first cousin to bologna and of course we eat bologna—or do we still eat it?—as it's sliced. I used to get a slice of bologna when I went to the butcher shop with my mother; it used to keep me quiet.

- 1 can (1 lb.) kidney beans
- 2 cups sliced frankfurters (7 to 8 frankfurters)
- ¾ cup sliced sour pickles
- ¾ cup French dressing
- 1 medium head lettuce
- ¼ large onion, sliced

Drain kidney beans. Add frankfurters, pickles, and ½ cup French dressing. Chill about 1 hour. Break lettuce leaves into pieces. Alternate layers of frankfurter mixture, lettuce, and onion in a shallow bowl. Pour the remaining French dressing over all. Garnish with a few onion rings. Chill. Makes 6 to 8 servings.

KIDNEY BEAN SALAD

2 cans (1 lb. each) kidney beans
½ cup diced celery
½ medium green pepper, cut in thin strips
½ medium onion, thinly sliced
2 slices canned pineapple, cubed
½ cup mayonnaise or salad dressing
½ teaspoon salt
⅛ teaspoon ground black pepper
Crisp lettuce
½ cup ripe olives
1 hard-cooked egg, sliced
1 tomato, sliced

Place beans into sieve; rinse with cold water; drain thoroughly. Combine beans, celery, green pepper, onion, pineapple, mayonnaise, salt, and pepper in mixing bowl; mix lightly until blended. Pile into lettuce-lined bowl or deep platter. Garnish top with olives, egg, and tomato. Makes 6 to 8 servings.

CELERIAC (CELERY ROOT) AND ORANGE SALAD

1 lb. celeriac (2 to 3 medium)
½ cup mayonnaise or salad dressing
2 tablespoons fresh lemon juice
1 tablespoon sugar
¼ teaspoon salt
Crisp salad greens
2 oranges, peeled and divided into sections
¼ cup coarsely chopped walnuts

Cut away and discard celeriac leaves and fibrous roots. Wash and scrub. Pare, cutting off woody covering. Shred on vegetable shredder. Mix together celeriac, mayonnaise, lemon juice, sugar, and salt. Heap onto crisp salad greens. Arrange orange sections around celeriac. Sprinkle walnuts on top. Makes 4 servings.

MELON AND BLACKBERRY SALAD

2 cups diced cantaloupe or honeydew melon, chilled
1 cup blackberries, picked over, washed, drained, chilled
1 cup finely diced celery, chilled
⅓ cup French dressing
½ teaspoon salt
Crisp salad greens
½ cup commercial sour cream

Lightly mix together melon, berries, celery, dressing, and salt, tossing until blended. Turn onto salad greens. Garnish with spoonfuls of sour cream. Makes 6 servings.

SNAPPY COLE SLAW

When I found this recipe many years ago, little did I dream that I'd be making it for television audiences. I consider this my personal treasure recipe. What happens is, the salt coaxes out cabbage moisture. When you squeeze, the result is dry cabbage strands, so thirsty they absorb that spicy mixture of olive oil, wine vinegar, and seasoning. Thus their flavors are in the cabbage strands. Even when the slaw stands over night in the refrigerator it doesn't get watery. Don't you feel great when you can take a plain ingredient like cabbage and turn it into something that's real gourmet? This is a gourmet recipe—yet one would never expect cabbage to be gourmet—but gourmet it is and we'll let it go at that. Two things my inner circle always requested of me when coming to my house to eat, and they were this Snappy Cole Slaw and the Dreamy Creamy Potato Salad. Two homespun dishes that are perfectly elegant. If I had to write a cookbook and include only three recipes I still believe I'd include this Snappy Cole Slaw, the Million Dollar Cheese Cake, and my Dreamy Creamy Potato Salad.

1 tablespoon salt
1 quart finely shredded cabbage
½ cup olive oil
2 cloves garlic, mashed
⅓ cup wine vinegar
½ cup minced parsley
1 small green pepper, minced

Sprinkle salt over cabbage; stir and let stand 15 minutes. Rub cabbage together, squeezing to bruise and make juices flow. Squeeze cabbage dry, discarding salty juice. Mix together olive oil, garlic, vinegar, parsley, and green pepper; pour over prepared cabbage. Mix well and chill several hours. Makes approximately 6 servings.

NOTE: Serve topped with anchovies, or as a star of the antipasto, or with all kinds of sea foods.

DREAMY CREAMY POTATO SALAD

Potatoes, any cook's good standby, are one of my favorite foods, and a joy to cook any style. It's no secret that they are the country's favorite vegetable, quoting from the U.S. Department of Agriculture's Agricultural Marketing Service.

Many varieties of potatoes reach the market all year long, each with a slight variation in texture and cooking quality. To be sure, we all know the Idaho baking potato is just right for baking, always dry and mealy, never wet and soggy. Unless one makes a mental note of the cooking qualities of previously used spuds, the shopper looking to buy potatoes needs a crystal ball. Only experts could tell from the outside whether they will cook moist and waxy or dry and mealy. The industry has started packaging potatoes with descriptive labels and promises that in the future all of them will be clearly marked as suitable for mashing, frying, salad-making, etc. Unless I've had experience with a particular type of potato, I test a batch by boiling one or two before making potato salad or any other dish where the results are important. In order to have unbroken slices or cubes of potatoes in salad, here's a preliminary precaution I've found works very well. After the unpeeled potatoes of various sizes are washed and ready for the saucepan, I always put the largest ones on the bottom, and add the remainder in graduated sizes, with the smallest on top; then cook them in boiling salted water. As the potatoes boil, the smallest ones cook first and can be lifted out while the bigger ones keep on cooking until done. This way none of the smaller ones will crack open and become water-logged while waiting for the larger ones to get tender. Simple? It makes quite a difference.

2 lbs. (6 to 8 medium) potatoes
¼ cup olive oil
¼ cup wine vinegar
¾ teaspoon salt
⅛ teaspoon ground black pepper
⅓ cup cold water
¾ cup mayonnaise or salad dressing
⅓ cup grated onion
½ cup finely chopped parsley

Cook unpared potatoes in slightly salted water to cover, until barely tender. Drain, peel, slice, or dice and set aside. Mix together oil, vinegar, salt, pepper, and cold water. Gradually stir mixture into mayonnaise. Stir in onion and parsley. Pour over potatoes, mixing lightly but well. Refrigerate to 2 hours or longer, until potatoes have absorbed most of the dressing. Makes approximately 6 to 8 servings.

NOTE: This is superb and does not dry out; potatoes do not stick together on standing.

FLORIDA GREEN AND GOLD SALAD

4 seedless oranges
2 grapefruit
Lettuce or other crisp salad greens
Crisp sprigs of mint
French Dressing

Peel oranges and grapefruit. Divide into sections and remove outer membrane. Arrange lettuce leaves, one inside the other, to form cups. Place on salad plate and fill lettuce cups with orange and grapefruit sections. Garnish with crisp sprigs of mint. Serve with French dressing. Makes 4 to 6 servings.

NOTE: In place of lettuce, two crisp leaves of romaine for each salad, arranged with one leaf inside of the other, make a very pretty elongated, boat-shaped salad. Garnish with crisp mint at each end.

BANANA SPLIT SALAD

- 1 pint cottage cheese
- 1 cup canned pineapple tid-bits, drained
- 4 ripe bananas, flecked with brown
- Crisp lettuce leaves
- 4 red maraschino cherries
- ¼ cup nuts, coarsely chopped
- 4 tablespoons mayonnaise or salad dressing

Mix thoroughly cottage cheese and pineapple tid-bits. Peel and split fully ripe bananas lengthwise. Place 1 or more crisp lettuce leaves on each of 4 salad plates. Arrange 2 banana halves, side by side, cut sides up, on top of lettuce on each plate. Place rounded spoons of cheese mixture on top of banana halves. Garnish each salad with cherry and nuts. Pass mayonnaise. Makes 4 servings.

NOTE: A teen-ager's delight for luncheon or a party.

9. *Desserts*

Dear Josie—Dear Josie—Dear Josie—My Pies!!—I can't make a good pie no matter how I try!! The crust is soggy underneath!—The apple pie I make with loving care comes out like a circus tent—the top crust way up high—then a big space and the apples down in the bottom of the pie—etc., etc., etc.

The wails about pie making coming my way via the mail bag would make a year-long screech. Yes, it's an old, old complaint and I hardly know where to begin. All I can tell you is try and try and try again until you hit upon it. I promise—scout's honor—once you get it right there will be no trouble. Furthermore, I wager that you'll find pie baking the most fun. Could even be that you'll win a gold medal for your pies if you ever compete in a pie baking contest.

Now if I were doing this on TV, you'd probably want to take notes for further reference. Now, however, you'll be saved the bother, as here it is in black and white. Herewith your questions and my answers from personal observations. Oh yes! I've long hurdled the pitfalls of pie-making and boldly call myself an "A No. 1" pie maker under any conditions and in any oven.

How to get a "flaky" crust. For a 2-crust pie, allow 2 cups sifted flour (sifted with 1 teaspoon salt), 3/4 cup chilled shortening, and 6 tablespoons ice water. Cut the shortening into the flour and salt mixture with two knives until the particles of fat are the size of large peas; don't rub together or use the hands. There should be dry flour all around the fat particles. Sprinkle water on top; toss lightly; press together and pat into a flattened ball. Then roll out and make your pie. Bake in a 425°F. hot oven. If the oven temperature is high enough, it will bake the crust and trap the pieces of fat before they have time to melt and seep evenly through the dough. The little particles of fat will melt in small trapped places of baked or "set" crust and produce flakiness.

Why the hollow apple pie? Tough pie crust, very soft apples, and over-baking can produce the hollow apple pie. Some apples shrink more than others in baking. If you know you're using soft tender apples, cook them with the sugar and spices first, but only enough to heat them through and shrink them; let them cool; then use them as your pie filling. Don't overbake. All apples shrink during cooking. They keep on shrinking as you bake them after they are tender. Time the pies in the oven; don't forget the apples keep on cooking and softening for a few minutes after the pie comes out of the oven and while it stays piping hot. I'm very careful about the apples I choose for apple pie. I pick firm, juicy apples that I know from experience.

How about underdone crusts in fruit pies? First, choose a dull-finish pie pan. Shiny pans reflect heat. Dull-finish pans absorb heat. You'll want the heat to penetrate the pie pan and begin to crisp the crust as soon as possible, not to be reflected away from the crust by the shiny pan surface. Help the crust to be moisture repellant. Before putting in the moist fruit filling, brush the crust with cooled melted butter or margarine; refrigerate it long enough to firm the fat; then add the filling. This protects the crust long enough for it to crisp before the fruit begins to boil. Always place a fruit pie nearer the bottom of the oven and in the hottest spot. If necessary, move it higher to brown the top when the pie is about half-baked.

How about custard pie? It's impossible to bake custard in a pie crust and have the bottom crust crisp. The only way to achieve this is to bake the custard in an identical size pie pan; then, just before serving, slip the pie-shaped baked custard into the crisp baked shell. Yes! It can be done, and easily, too, with a little practice. I've done it on television several times with all eyes on me and under tension, with the Director's distracting speed-up cues. Just take a firm grip on your pans and yourself and let-er-fly! Even if the custard cracks the first time or so, it's still edible and delicious! Master it you will! Keep trying! As Harriet van Horne says, "Just one more time."

Why does the crisp baked crust under my finished lemon meringue pie get so soggy? Blame here goes to the meringue. "Weepy" meringue "weeps" tears of syrup that seep into the chip-dry thirsty baked crust—so look to your meringue. It takes 2 tablespoons sugar and a speck of salt for each egg white to whip up a nice silky meringue. The sugar crystals beaten with the egg whites must be completely dissolved.

Egg whites should be at room temperature. Add the salt and ⅓ of the sugar as soon as the egg whites begin to froth as you beat. Beat until foamy and add the second part of the sugar. The last third of the sugar should go in soon after, giving the sugar all that dissolving time while you beat the mixture to the "peak" stage. Pour cooled-to-lukewarm pie filling into crispy baked pie crust. Spread the silky meringue on top. Bake long enough to cook the egg white. It can be baked in a 400°F. hot oven about 7 minutes—or baked in a 325°F. slow oven 14 to 16 minutes. Either way works well, and I use both ways.

While pie crust needs high heat the moment it goes into the oven to form a brittle crust as soon as possible, a cake needs moderate heat to allow the cake to rise before a rigid crust forms on the outside. That's the reason shiny pans, which are taboo for pies, reflecting heat away from them as they do, are desirable for cake baking. Yes, a gal needs her pie pans to be dull to bake a good pie—and she needs her cake pans to be shiny in order to bake a fine cake.

◆§ CHOCOLATE YEAST CAKE

The telephones kept up a constant din for this recipe. Mysterious yeast, the ingredient most women never tackle, because of fear, actually worked on TV. They could see the beautiful cake. I explained how it stayed moist and tender for such a long time too. Letters poured in requesting the recipe. Personally, I think yeast dough is great fun to handle. You can't help having a light cake or bread when you use yeast. Over and over I've been explaining via TV and by letter that with yeast you have to wait and give the yeast a chance to grow. As it grows, it leavens the cake or bread. This means it fills the cake with skillions of tiny gas cells. Then, in baking, the gas escapes and air rushes in. Result—a lovely porous cake. Southerners still call yeast breads or rolls, light bread. They've got to be light. The recipe guides you to use warm or lukewarm, not hot, water to soften yeast. Know why? Hot water would make the yeast inactive, and no matter how long you waited, nothing would happen. That is the only real precaution. Not to use hot water is the first step. The recipe says to keep the dough warm. "How do you keep it warm?" women wail. Know what I tell them? "If you don't have a warm spot—make one. Turn the oven to low heat. Wrap up the bowl of mixed yeast dough. Put it on a stool near the open oven door. That failing, put the bowl down into a large pot of warm water. Keep changing the water as it cools. Then wait the prescribed time. You don't have to sit and watch it either. Set your timer and go about your household chores. The results will be sheer magic." I do believe that once you've had a yeast-made cake turn out fine and dandy, you'll say to yourself, "Josie's right—baking with yeast is more fun than anything. Besides, just notice the wonderful smell it sends all through the house." Yes, It's a grand aroma; translated it means "HOME IS HEAVEN when Mom bakes with yeast."

1 package active dry yeast
¼ cup warm (not hot) water
¾ cup milk, scalded, then cooled to lukewarm
1 tablespoon sugar
2 cups sifted all-purpose flour
2 cups sugar
¾ cup soft butter or margarine
⅔ cup cocoa
½ cup water
3 eggs, beaten
1 cup sifted all-purpose flour
1 teaspoon baking soda
½ teaspoon salt
1 teaspoon pure vanilla extract
1 cup raisins

Sprinkle yeast onto warm (not hot) water in large bowl. Stir until dissolved. Add milk, 1 tablespoon sugar, and 2 cups flour; beat smooth. Cover with clean towel and let rise in warm place (about 85°F.) about 45 minutes, or until mixture is light and spongy. Meanwhile, stir sugar into butter and set aside. Combine cocoa and water in top of double boiler; place over hot water and cook, stirring constantly for about 5 minutes, or until thick and smooth. Cool. Add butter and cooled cocoa mixtures to yeast mixture. Add eggs, remaining flour, baking soda, salt, and vanilla. Beat by hand 8 to 10 minutes, or 6 minutes on electric mixer at low speed, or until smooth. Add raisins and blend. Pour into 2 greased, waxed paper-lined 9 x 9 x 1¾-inch square cake pans. Let rise in warm place (85°F.) about 30 to 35 minutes or until doubled in bulk. Bake in a moderate oven (350°F.) about 30 to 35 minutes or until done. Cool in pans on rack. Frost with Honey Nut Frosting. Makes 2 (9-inch) square layers.

Honey Nut Frosting

2 egg whites, unbeaten
¾ cup sugar
1 tablespoon cold water
½ cup honey
¼ teaspoon cream of tartar
¼ teaspoon salt
½ cup chopped walnuts or pecans

Combine egg whites, sugar, water, honey, cream of tartar, and salt in top of double boiler. Blend with electric mixer at high speed about 1 minute. Place over galloping boiling water. Continue beating at high speed about 6 to 7 minutes or until peaks form upon raising the beater. Remove from heat and beat until thick enough to spread. Add nuts and blend. Makes enough frosting for 2 layers.

◆§ STRAWBERRY DREAM CAKE

I had heard about this cake from one of my food editor friends and I went searching until I found the recipe. And after I made it, I decided that here was a cake that you just couldn't skip, and the audience went mad about it. The recipe requests for this poured in by the thousands! As a matter of fact, some people months later still thought of it, and asked for that Dreamy Strawberry Cake. And dreamy is just half of it! I think I could eat a whole cake myself!

1 cup plus 2 tablespoons sifted self-rising cake flour
or 1 cup sifted all-purpose flour
2 teaspoons baking powder
½ teaspoon salt
½ cup soft butter or margarine
½ cup sugar
3 egg yolks
1 teaspoon pure vanilla extract
¼ cup milk
1 cup sliced strawberries or whole raspberries, fresh or frozen
3 egg whites, at room temperature
¼ cup sugar
1 cup heavy cream, whipped and sweetened to taste
Whole berries to garnish

If self-rising flour is used, omit baking powder and salt. If all-purpose flour is used, sift together with baking powder and salt and set aside. Beat butter or margarine until creamy. Gradually add sugar, beating until fluffy. Fold in egg yolks and vanilla and beat until fluffy. Gradually add self-rising cake flour or all-purpose flour mixture alternately with milk, mixing only until blended. Turn into 2 well-greased, waxed-paper-lined and then greased 8-inch layer cake pans. Spread berries evenly over batter. Beat egg whites until frothy; gradually add remaining sugar, beating until stiff, shiny peaks form. Spread evenly over berries to the edges of the pan. Bake in a moderate oven (350°F.) 35 to 40 minutes or until done. Cool about 10 minutes before removing from pan. When cool, invert one layer onto the other so that two cake tops are together with their topping forming the filling. Frost with sweetened whipped cream and garnish with additional whole berries if desired. Makes 1 (8-inch) layer cake.

☙ MILLION DOLLAR CHEESE CAKE

Here's hoping you eat this cheese cake with reverence. It has brought so much pleasure. This is a recipe I took with me to England when I was invited over there by the British Dairy Council for the equivalent of our American Dairy Council's June Dairy Month to launch their June Dairy Cookery promotion. Yes, they started the same kind of June promotion to encourage the use of cheese and the drinking of milk such as we have here. Fluffy cheese cake is getting so popular in this country that when folks from the Middle West come East, one of the things they all expect to eat is New York cheese cake. Many of them take the recipe back home. Before we know it cheese cake will be as popular as apple pie!

You can hardly go wrong on this. There's only one precaution, and that is to take it out of the oven while it's still slightly soft in the middle, because it will be grainy textured, not smooth, if you overcook it. This is a moist delicate cake and—my goodness—is it ever delicious! I often make this instead of a birthday cake for birthday parties and put the candles right down into the cheese cake. My guests are always so grateful! I've been tempted to go in business for myself—manufacturing just this one cake!

- 1⅓ cups fine graham cracker crumbs (about 16 crackers)
- ¼ cup sugar
- ¼ cup soft butter or margarine
- 5 egg yolks
- ½ cup sugar
- 1½ lbs. softened cream cheese
- 1 teaspoon grated lemon rind
- 5 egg whites
- ½ teaspoon salt
- ½ cup sugar

Combine graham cracker crumbs, sugar, and butter. Rub together or blend until crumbly. Press mixture firmly onto entire insides of well-greased 8-inch spring-form pan and set aside. Beat egg yolks until very thick; gradually add ½ cup sugar; continue beating until fluffy. Mash cream cheese until smooth and add to egg yolk mixture with lemon rind. Mix thoroughly. Beat egg whites and salt until soft mounds begin to form. Add ½ cup sugar, 2 tablespoons at a time; continue beating until stiff peaks are formed. Fold into egg yolk-cream cheese mixture until thoroughly blended. Turn mixture into crumb-lined spring-form pan. Bake in a moderate oven (350°F.) about 45 to 50 minutes or until cake is done. Cool on rack. Makes 1 (8-inch) cake.

UPSIDE DOWN PEACH CAKE

We made this using cherries and peaches and it was a picture. Before the show was off the air the phone calls began to pour in with questions from women who wanted to know if they could use plums or apricots or any other fruits. Yes, indeed you can, preparing the pan exactly the same way. Same amount of brown sugar and same amount of butter and the same amount of batter for the same size pan, of course, and just place the fruit always with the side down that you want to be uppermost. If you want to use sliced fruit, just place the slices down flat. Don't forget the way you place them down; if you could look up through the pan, that will be the top of the cake. My advice to you is not to be nervous when you turn the cake over. Attack it boldly. After you have put the serving plate over the cake, put the palm of one hand on top and the palm of the other hand underneath and just turn it over. Don't lift the pan off right away. Let it set a minute and steam.

- 1/3 cup soft butter or margarine
- 1/2 cup sifted brown sugar, packed
- 10 to 12 maraschino cherries
- 10 to 12 fresh peeled or well-drained canned peach halves
- Upside Down Cake Batter

Spread soft butter evenly over bottom of 9 x 9 x 1¾-inch cake pan. Sprinkle with brown sugar. Place maraschino cherries in peach-pit hollows. Arrange peaches rounded-side up over brown sugar. Cover with Upside Down Cake Batter (see below). Bake in a moderate oven (350°F.) about 45 minutes or until cake is done. Remove from oven, loosen cake all around sides of pan with knife or spatula. Place serving plate over cake and invert at once, peach-side up. Let stand two minutes. Lift off pan. Serve warm or cold. Makes 1 (9-inch) square cake.

Upside Down Cake Batter

- 1 cup sifted all-purpose flour
- 1 teaspoon baking powder
- 1/2 teaspoon salt
- 2 eggs
- 2/3 cup sugar
- 6 tablespoons any fruit juice
- 1 teaspoon pure vanilla extract

Sift together flour, baking powder, and salt; set aside. Beat eggs until light. Gradually add sugar; continue beating until thick and fine grained. Stir in fruit juice and vanilla. Gradually add sifted dry ingredients, folding in only until all the flour has been dampened. Pour over fruit and bake as above.

◆ OLD-FASHIONED LEMON LAYER CAKE

- 1½ cups sifted all-purpose flour
- 1 cup sugar
- 2½ teaspoons double-acting baking powder
- ½ teaspoon salt
- ½ cup shortening
- ½ cup milk
- 2 eggs
- 1 teaspoon pure vanilla extract
- Confectioners' sugar

Sift together flour, sugar, baking powder, and salt into mixing bowl. Add shortening, ⅔ of the milk, 1 egg, and vanilla. Beat 2 minutes at low speed with electric mixer or 2 minutes by hand. Scrape down bowl and beater two or three times during mixing. Add remaining milk and egg. Beat 2 minutes, scraping bowl and beater after 1 minute of beating. Turn into 2 well-greased and floured 8-inch layer cake pans. Bake in a moderate oven (350°F.) about 25 minutes or until cakes are done. Cool. Put together with Lemon Filling. Sprinkle with sugar. Makes 1 (8-inch) cake.

Lemon Filling

- 7 tablespoons cornstarch
- ¾ cup sugar
- ¼ teaspoon salt
- 1½ cups hot water
- 3 egg yolks, beaten
- ½ cup sugar
- 2 tablespoons butter or margarine
- ½ cup fresh lemon juice
- 1 teaspoon grated lemon rind
- ¼ teaspoon pure vanilla extract

Mix together cornstarch, ¾ cup sugar, and salt in saucepan. Add hot water gradually. Bring to boiling temperature and cook about 7 minutes or until thickened and clear, stirring constantly. Combine egg yolks and remaining sugar in bowl. Gradually add hot mixture, stirring constantly. Return to saucepan, add butter, and cook 3 to 4 minutes, stirring as before. Remove from heat. Gradually stir in lemon juice, rind, and vanilla. Cool and chill.

❧ LAZY DAZY PRUNELLA CAKE

This recipe was sent in by one of the viewers. After testing and retesting, it was finally made to work and it made a beautiful loaf of cake, pretty enough for a color picture. It sounds too easy to be true. Imagine not having to cream the butter or whip the eggs or do any folding. Just measure everything one on top of the other and then mix. Outside of having to measure the ingredients, it's just about the easiest cake going yet—because there's no mixing time on it, there's not a word about "beat so many strokes" or so many minutes on this speed or that speed. What could be simpler? And this is such a rich moist cake—you don't need to frost it at all. It's terrific for lunch boxes or picnic baskets and the last word with ice-cream on the side, or spooned on top. Oh yes, it stays moist for such a long time. It's a versatile recipe. You can add nuts if you like, or reduce the amount of prunes and add a few raisins. The dear lady who took the trouble to send me in the original recipe has an everlasting place in my heart.

- ½ cup soft butter or shortening
- 1 cup sugar
- 2 eggs, beaten
- 1⅓ cups sifted all-purpose flour
- ½ teaspoon baking powder
- ½ teaspoon baking soda
- ½ teaspoon salt
- ½ teaspoon ground nutmeg
- ½ teaspoon ground cinnamon
- ½ teaspoon ground allspice
- ½ cup buttermilk
- ⅔ cup pitted cooked dried prunes
- 1 teaspoon pure vanilla extract

Place butter in mixing bowl. Place sugar and eggs on top without mixing. Sift together flour, baking powder, baking soda, salt, and spices and add. Do not mix. Place buttermilk, prunes, and vanilla on top. Mix well. Turn into greased, waxed-paper-lined 10 x 5 x 3-inch loaf pan. Bake in a moderate oven (350°F.) 45 to 50 minutes or until cake is done. Makes 1 large loaf.

⌘ BANANA CHIFFON CAKE

- 2¼ cups sifted cake flour
- 1½ cups sugar
- 1 tablespoon double-acting baking powder
- 1 teaspoon salt
- ½ cup salad oil
- 5 medium-size egg yolks, unbeaten
- 1 cup mashed ripe bananas (2 to 3 bananas)
- 1 tablespoon fresh lemon juice
- ½ teaspoon cream of tartar
- 1 cup egg whites (7 or 8)

Sift together flour, sugar, baking powder, and salt into mixing bowl. Make a "well" in dry ingredients and add, in order, oil, egg yolks, bananas, and lemon juice. Beat until smooth. Add cream of tartar to egg whites. Beat egg whites in a large mixing bowl until they form very stiff peaks. Do NOT UNDERBEAT. Gradually and gently fold banana mixture into egg whites, just until blended. Do NOT STIR. Pour into ungreased, 10-inch tube pan, 4 inches deep. Bake in a moderate oven (325°F.) about 1 hour and 5 minutes, or until cake is done. Immediately turn pan upside down, placing the tube part over a small-necked bottle or funnel so that the pan is elevated about 1 inch above surface of table. Let cake hang until cold. Loosen cake from sides and tube of pan with spatula. Turn pan over and tap edge sharply to loosen cake. Spread top and sides of cake with your favorite frosting, if desired. Makes 1 (10-inch) cake —8 to 12 servings.

☙ AVGOKALAMARA (FRIED GREEK TEA CAKES)

These are superb! And here's where you can use your imagination, using some other nuts besides the walnuts, or adding liqueurs or spices or herbs to the honey sauce that goes over them, and create a name for yourself as an exotic cook! Although these have a mysterious sounding Greek name, if you'll look over the recipe you'll see that the ingredients called for are all in your house, excepting maybe the nuts—and you could substitute, well, something like caraway seed for the walnuts in the syrup.

2 cups sifted all-purpose flour
½ teaspoon baking powder
½ teaspoon salt
2 eggs, beaten
¼ cup fresh orange juice
1 teaspoon fresh lemon juice
Oil for shallow-frying
¾ cup honey
¼ cup water
¾ cup finely chopped walnuts
Ground cinnamon

Sift together flour, baking powder, and salt. Combine eggs, orange and lemon juice in mixing bowl. Beat well. Gradually add sifted dry ingredients, stirring until blended. Turn out on lightly floured surface and knead until smooth. Divide dough in half. Work with one half at a time; roll out ⅛ inch thick. Cut into ½-inch-by-3½-inch strips, using a pastry wheel or knife. Tie strips loosely to make knots; make different shapes if desired. Fry 4 to 6 at a time without crowding, in about 2 inches of oil heated to 370°F., about 2 minutes or until golden, turning once. Lift out and let drain on absorbent paper. Repeat with remaining half of dough. Combine honey and water in saucepan; bring to a boil. Fill deep platter with alternate layers of fried avgokalamaras, honey mixture, nuts, and cinnamon.

Spoon sauce in platter over cakes as they cool. Eat with fingers. Makes about 3 to 3½ dozen.

◆§ ONE-PAN CRUMB COFFEE CAKE

Imagine making cake when you don't have to mess up bowls! This is for me! This is a crumb topping that stays on top of the cake. The telephone calls that come in yelling, "My crumbs all disappeared!" . . . Well, this is the answer. Try this crumb topping and stick to the recipe. Don't try to add more butter or margarine just because you want to make it richer. That's what causes the trouble! Too much shortening!

1 cup plus 2 tablespoons self-rising cake flour
or 1 cup plus 2 tablespoons sifted cake flour
2 teaspoons baking powder
½ teaspoon salt
¼ cup butter or margarine
⅓ cup sugar
1 egg
Milk
1 teaspoon pure vanilla extract
1 recipe Crumb Topping

If self-rising flour is used, omit baking powder and salt. If cake flour is used, sift together with baking powder and salt into mixing bowl. Melt butter in 8-inch round cake pan. Add sugar and stir in thoroughly, using a fork. Place flour on top of sugar mixture. Break egg into measuring cup and stir in enough milk to make ¾ cup. Add vanilla. Pour into pan over flour. Stir until flour is dampened. Do not expect an entirely smooth batter as there will be a few tiny lumps remaining even after flour disappears. Sprinkle evenly with Crumb Topping (recipe below). Bake in a moderate oven (350°F.) 25 minutes, or until done. Makes 1 (8-inch) cake.

Crumb Topping

½ cup plus 2 tablespoons sifted all-purpose flour
⅓ cup confectioners' sugar
2 tablespoons fine dry bread crumbs
2 tablespoons soft butter or margarine
1 teaspoon ground cinnamon
¼ teaspoon ground nutmeg

Combine all ingredients; rub together or blend until crumbly. Spread evenly over unbaked cake.

NO-FLOUR STRAWBERRY MERINGUE LAYER CAKE

The Layers

1⅓ cups egg whites (about 12 medium whites), at room temperature
¼ teaspoon salt
1 teaspoon pure vanilla extract
1½ cups granulated sugar

The Filling

1 cup heavy cream, whipped
1 cup sliced sweetened fresh strawberries
1 cup whole fresh strawberries, with stems on

Beat egg whites with salt until frothy. Add vanilla; add sugar, 2 tablespoons at a time, continuing beating with electric mixer at medium speed until stiff peaks are formed. Spread evenly into 2 ungreased 9-inch spring form pans; level tops with spatula dipped in cold water. Bake in a slow oven (275°F.) about 50 minutes or until done; cool on rack. Loosen layers all around sides with spatula; remove spring form sides. Gently slide one meringue layer off onto cake plate. Spread half the cream on this bottom layer; spoon sliced berries on top. Ease remaining layer off spring form bottom and place on top of berries. Cover with remaining whipped cream. Press whole strawberries lightly into cream. Chill about 1 hour before serving. To cut easily, dip knife in hot water. Makes 1 (9-inch) layer cake.

SUGARLESS SPONGE CAKE ROLL

- 6 egg whites, at room temperature
- ½ teaspoon salt
- 6 egg yolks
- ½ cup sifted all-purpose flour
- 1½ cups dietetic jam or jelly (made without sugar)

Beat egg whites with salt until soft mounds begin to form. Using the same beater, unwashed, beat egg yolks until thick and lemon-colored. Fold into egg whites. Sift in flour, folding in gently but thoroughly. Turn into prepared (see note) 15½-x-10½-inch jelly roll pan. Bake in a slow oven (325°F.) about 18 minutes, until pale golden in color and beginning to shrink away from sides of pan. Invert at once onto floured paper slightly larger than pan. Thinly slice off crisp edges all around cake to prevent cracking when rolling. Spread with dietetic jam or jelly. Roll up tight lengthwise from side to side and let rest one hour or longer on seam. Slice 1 to 1¼ inch thick. Makes 10 to 12 slices.

NOTE: To prepare pan, spread generously with mixture of 5 tablespoons unsalted shortening and 1 tablespoon flour. No paper lining is needed when this is used to coat insides of pan.

APPLE RIBBON PIE

6 to 8 large tart apples
Pastry for 2-crust pie
1 cup sugar
1 tablespoon flour
¼ teaspoon ground nutmeg
½ teaspoon ground cinnamon
2 tablespoons butter or margarine
¼ cup grated sharp cheddar cheese
1½ teaspoons poppy seed

Pare and core apples; slice thin. Line 9-inch pie pan with pastry. Combine sugar, flour, and spices; rub a little of this mixture into pastry in pie pan. Fill pie pan with sliced apples; add remaining sugar mixture. Dot with butter or margarine. Divide remaining pastry into 2 equal portions. Roll out 1 portion ⅛ inch thick; top with grated cheese; fold over in 3 layers; roll out again. Cut into 5 strips 10 inches long by ¾ inch wide. Repeat with remaining portion of pastry, using poppy seed instead of cheese. Weave strips, lattice fashion, on pie; trim and flute edge. Bake in hot oven (425°F.) 40 to 45 minutes, or until apples are tender. Makes one (9-inch) pie.

RHUBARB PIE

This pie was *such* a treat. Rhubarb pie is juicy; the juice should be slightly thickened and glossy, but still runny. The measured amount of tapioca took care of this perfectly. Notice how the bottom crust was brushed with melted butter, and chilled before filling. Sometimes I brush unbeaten egg white on the undercrust and let it dry. Either way keeps the juicy fruit filling from soaking into the undercrust long enough for the oven heat to set and bake it. I often recommend a pie-baking session in which you make not just one pie to be eaten right away, but two or three extra to freeze unbaked to enjoy in the future. The unbaked frozen pies should be carefully covered on top with a paper plate, then freezer wrapped and stored in a freezer that holds a temperature of zero or below. They can be baked frozen or thawed with good results. To bake unthawed or frozen pies, put them into a hot oven (425°F.); start the pie near the bottom of the oven; allow about 25 minutes more baking time or until top and bottom are browned and pie is bubbling in the center. Don't forget to slit top crust for steam vent. Take care lest top crust gets brown before the pie is baked through.

1½ cups sugar
¼ teaspoon salt
3 tablespoons quick-cooking tapioca
4 cups diced rhubarb unpeeled
Pastry for 9-inch double crust pie
1 tablespoon melted butter or margarine

Mix together sugar, salt, tapioca, and rhubarb. Set aside while pastry is being made. Line 9-inch pie pan with pastry rolled ⅛ inch thick; brush with melted butter and chill. Fill chilled pastry with rhubarb mixture and dot with remaining butter. Moisten edges of pastry with cold water and adjust top crust. Make several slits in top crust for escape of steam. Brush top with milk or egg white. Bake in a hot oven (425°F.) 50 minutes or until done. Makes 1 (9-inch) double crust pie.

Rich Flaky Pastry
(For 9-inch Double-Crust Pie)

2 cups sifted all-purpose flour
½ teaspoon salt
1 cup chilled shortening
5 to 6 tablespoons ice water

Sift together flour and salt into mixing bowl. Add shortening. Cut in with 2 knives; criss-cross or blend until fat is size of large corn kernels. Sprinkle on water while tossing with fork to form crumbs. Press crumbs together until dough forms. Press into a ball on lightly floured surface and roll out as directed.

FROZEN LEMON PIE

3 egg yolks
¼ cup fresh lemon juice
⅛ teaspoon salt
½ cup sugar
2 teaspoons grated lemon rind
3 egg whites
1 tablespoon sugar
1 cup heavy cream, whipped
¾ cup vanilla wafer crumbs

Beat egg yolks until thick. Stir in lemon juice, salt, and sugar. Turn into top of double boiler and place over gently boiling water. Cook, stirring constantly until mixture thickens and coats the spoon. Remove from heat. Stir in lemon rind and turn into mixing bowl. Cool. Beat egg whites until frothy. Add 1 tablespoon sugar and beat until stiff peaks form. Fold into cooled egg yolk mixture. Fold in whipped cream until thoroughly blended. Sprinkle ½ cup vanilla wafer crumbs over bottom of greased 9-inch pie pan. Spread pie filling over the crumbs and sprinkle remaining crumbs on top. Freeze several hours or until firm. Serve frozen; cut into wedges. Makes 1 (9-inch) pie.

About those vanilla wafer crumbs—actually, the crumbs can be from any kind of cookies you have in the house, even graham crackers. And about crushing them, I find if you just put them into a paper bag and run the rolling pin over them a few times, you get nice fine crumbs; or you can crush them in a modern electric blender, and then you won't have a mess to clean up. About how long to freeze the pie? Well, it's hard to tell you because different freezers have different efficiency. It might freeze in some freezers in an hour; it might take three hours in another. By the way, this would be a wonderful pie to make the night before or the day before. I've often made two or three ahead of time and served them for a party or a group. These keep very well, and if you gals have one of the large deep freezers, well, you could keep these—oh, weeks! And enjoy them at some future time for an impromptu party.

◆§ TWO CRUST LEMON PIE

This proved to be one of the most popular recipes I ever did. The reason, I think, is that a two-crust lemon pie has baffled a good many home bakers for a long time. This one really works, and it's creamy and lively and I think perfectly delicious. You really should try this; it's a change.

- 1½ cups sifted all-purpose flour
- ½ teaspoon salt
- 1 tablespoon sugar
- ½ cup chilled shortening
- 4 tablespoons milk
- 1 tablespoon cornstarch
- 1 cup sugar
- ¼ teaspoon salt
- 3 eggs, well-beaten
- 2 tablespoons melted butter or margarine
- ⅓ cup fresh lemon juice
- 3 tablespoons water
- 1 teaspoon grated lemon rind

Sift together flour, salt, and sugar into mixing bowl; add shortening; blend or cut in with two knives until like fine meal. Sprinkle milk evenly over mixture, tossing with fork until dough clings to fork. Turn onto lightly floured board. Press into a ball, roll lightly until smooth, and divide in half. Line a 9-inch pie pan with half the dough. Mix together cornstarch, sugar, and salt; stir into eggs. Stir in melted butter, lemon juice, water, and lemon rind. Mix thoroughly. Pour into pastry-lined pie pan. Roll out remaining dough slightly larger than pan and transfer over filling. Seal and flute edges. Prick top with a fork for escape of steam. Brush with milk. Bake in a hot oven (400°F.) about 35 minutes, or until done. Cool and chill before cutting. Makes one (9-inch) pie.

FRESH STRAWBERRY OR RASPBERRY CREAM TORTE

The Pastry

1½ cups sifted all-purpose flour
1 tablespoon sugar
1 teaspoon salt
⅓ cup shortening
1 egg yolk
5 tablespoons milk

The Filling

1½ cups milk
4 tablespoons cornstarch
⅓ cup sugar
¼ teaspoon salt
1 egg, beaten
½ cup milk
½ teaspoon pure vanilla extract

The Strawberry or Raspberry Glaze

2 tablespoons cornstarch
½ cup sugar
½ cup water
¼ teaspoon red food coloring, or to suit
2 cups (1 pint) hulled fresh strawberries or red raspberries, hulled

The Pastry: Sift together flour, sugar, and salt into mixing bowl; add shortening, rub together or blend until like coarse meal. Stir egg yolk into milk. Sprinkle over dry mixture. Mix well and shape into a ball. Roll dough ¼-inch thick on lightly floured surface. Lay flat bottom inset of 8-inch spring-form pan on dough and cut around it to make bottom crust. Lift cut out dough onto spring-form pan inset and clamp pan sides into place. Cut 2 x 4-inch strips from remaining dough. Fit dough strips around insides of spring form pan to meet the bottom dough, pressing the dough against the sides to make a shell; ease out any irregularities. Prick dough deep and close together on bottom and sides with a sharp fork. Chill about 1 hour, or until firm. Bake in a hot oven (400°F.) about 15 to 18 minutes or until golden brown and done. Cool.

The Filling: Heat 1½ cups milk to scalding in top of double boiler over gently boiling water. Combine cornstarch, sugar, salt, egg, and ½ cup milk in mixing bowl. Stir until blended. Gradually add the hot milk, stirring briskly. Return to double boiler and cook, stirring constantly, until thick and smooth, about 6 to 8 minutes. Add vanilla and cool. Cover to prevent skin forming on top.

The Strawberry or Raspberry Glaze: Combine cornstarch, half the sugar, and water in small saucepan and blend. Place over moderate heat; cook, stirring constantly until very thick, smooth, and clear. Add remaining sugar and red food coloring. Stir until sugar is dissolved. Remove from heat and cool until warm, but not set. Fold in whole berries.

To Finish the Torte: Spread cooled thick filling in baked pastry shell. Top with glazed berries. Chill 1 to 2 hours before cutting. Makes 1 (8-inch) torte.

◆§ OLD-FASHIONED CREAMY RICE PUDDING

This is a true old-fashioned creamy rice pudding recipe. The real he-man favorite. No diner across the 48 states dares to open its doors without having a great big pan of rice pudding all ready. I'll never forget a woman who had decided to open up an eating place in Connecticut. She wrote me an S.O.S. and said, "Josie, I can't find a recipe for Rice Pudding—the old-fashioned kind—in any book, high or low, that I've searched so far. Please, please send it to me!" I agree with this dear lady; the recipes for the old-fashioned things are kind of scarce—but here's one old-fashioned pudding that certainly shouldn't be shelved. What do you say we revive it. It certainly should make the rice people happy!

¼ cup raw regular rice, washed and drained
1 cup water
½ teaspoon salt
1 tablespoon butter or margarine
⅓ cup sugar
1 quart milk
½ cup raisins, parboiled 2 to 3 minutes and drained, or steamed until plump
Ground nutmeg

Place rice, water, and salt into small saucepan over high heat. Bring to a boil. Lower heat, cover tightly and let rice steam about 35 to 40 minutes or until soft and all water has been absorbed. Add butter, sugar, and milk to cooked rice; stir briskly and turn into greased 1½-quart casserole. Bake in a very slow oven (250°F.) about 2 hours, stirring the top skin down into the pudding as it forms at 15 or 20 minute intervals. Add raisins, if desired, 15 minutes before baking time is up. Do not stir after adding raisins. When final skin has formed on top at end of baking time, remove from oven; sprinkle nutmeg on top. Cool and chill thoroughly. Pudding will only thicken slightly when chilled 7 to

8 hours or longer. Makes 1 quart pudding, or about 8 servings.

◆§ BAKED PRUNE WHIP DAINTIES

You just couldn't have stood all day baking a fancy cake and have it get more raves than these innocent little prune whip dainties. They're almost an after-thought. You have eggs in the house, you have crackers in the house, you have prunes in the house. Go ahead and make some prune whip dainties for that crowd that's sitting around just daring you to break out with something elegant and fancy. So often the simple things please us the most. That's just what these are—simple to make and most pleasing to eat, and beautiful to look at!

- 3 egg whites, at room temperature
- 1 teaspoon fresh lemon juice
- 1 cup sugar
- 1 cup finely chopped pitted cooked dried prunes
- 2 dozen salted crackers

Beat egg whites and lemon juice until frothy. Gradually add sugar while continuing to beat until mixture stands in peaks. Fold in prunes. Spread thickly on crackers, piling mixture high. Bake in a moderate oven (350°F.) about 10 to 12 minutes or until puffed and brown. Serve hot. Makes about 2 dozen.

◆§ POTS DE CREME AU CHOCOLAT

This is a very rich dessert and we made it after we got so many requests last summer from women who evidently had been abroad and tasted it in some of the celebrated French restaurants. I always maintain that you don't have to go abroad to eat their specialties. We have everything in this wonderful country to reproduce them here, every bit as well as they make them. Don't forget they've been working at these things for a long time, and after you've made your recipes a few times you'll be just as expert as they.

2 cups heavy cream
3 tablespoons sugar
⅔ cup (4 oz.) semi-sweet chocolate morsels
½ teaspoon salt
5 egg yolks
2 teaspoons pure vanilla extract
Whipped cream for garnish

Combine cream, sugar, semi-sweet chocolate, and salt in top of double boiler over gently boiling water. Let heat to scalding, stirring frequently. Whip with rotary or electric hand beater until smooth and silky. Beat egg yolks until thick; gradually add hot mixture to egg yolks, stirring constantly. Return mixture to double boiler; cook about 1 or 2 minutes or long enough to cook the yolks, stirring constantly. Remove from heat. Add vanilla and pour into small special Pots de Creme pots or custard cups. Cool and chill about 3 hours or longer until thickened and jelly-like. Serve with whipped cream as garnish. Makes 6 servings.

☙ EGG WHITE CUP CUSTARD

¼ cup sugar
⅛ teaspoon salt
2 cups hot, not boiling, milk
½ cup or 4 egg whites
½ teaspoon pure vanilla extract
Ground nutmeg

Add sugar and salt to milk, stirring until sugar is dissolved. Beat egg whites until they begin to foam; gradually add milk. Mix thoroughly. Strain through a fine sieve to remove egg cords; add vanilla. Turn into 5 or 6 well-greased custard cups. Sprinkle nutmeg on top. Place cups into baking pan. Pour hot water into pan up to 1 inch below cup rims. Bake in a slow oven (325° F.) about 25 to 30 minutes or until set and mixture is no longer runny on testing with tip of knife inserted in the center. Lift custards out of hot water and cool. Makes 4 to 6 servings.

NOTE: This uses left-over egg whites.

☙ TOP-OF-THE-STOVE CUSTARD

You're going to say "Glory, Hallelujah!" about this recipe, because you don't have to light the oven to get a smooth, creamy custard. I know you won't believe it until you try it and see how well it turns out. This is steamed custard, so don't expect it to have any of the brownish patches that are sometimes on baked-in-the-oven custards. The trick is not to let the water boil up around it and not to overcook it—or you'll have a "weepy" custard. I'd start testing it at 15 minutes. Just insert the tip of a knife down in the center and, if it's still runny—if the knife comes out with milk clinging to it—you know that the custard needs a little more heating. When these custards are cold they'll turn out and stand up firm just like a custard that was baked in the oven. What a boon for a hot summer day when you want a homemade dessert and dread the thought of the oven heating up the kitchen!

2 to 4 tablespoons sugar
¼ teaspoon salt
2 cups hot, not boiling, milk
3 eggs, beaten
½ teaspoon pure vanilla extract
Ground nutmeg (optional)

Add sugar and salt to milk. Stir until sugar is dissolved. Stir into eggs. Add vanilla; mix well and pour into well-greased custard cups. Sprinkle with nutmeg. Stand filled cups in small amount of hot water in large skillet or frying pan. Pour more boiling water around cups up to 1 inch below rims. Place over low heat; cover and steam, without boiling, about 15 to 20 minutes or until centers of custards are no longer runny on testing with tip of a knife. Remove from heat; lift out custards and cool. Makes 5 to 6 servings.

ORANGE CHANTILLY PUDDING

- 1½ cups water
- ½ cup sugar
- ¼ cup quick-cooking tapioca
- ¼ teaspoon salt
- 1 cup fresh orange juice
- 1 teaspoon grated orange rind
- ¾ cup fresh orange sections
- ½ cup heavy cream, whipped

Combine water, sugar, tapioca, and salt in saucepan; mix well. Place over direct heat; cook about 3 to 4 minutes, stirring constantly. Remove from heat. Add orange juice and rind; mix well and cool. Chill until serving time. To serve, fold in ½ cup orange sections; lightly fold in whipped cream. Turn into individual or one large serving dish. Garnish top with remaining orange sections. Makes 6 servings.

COTTAGE CHEESE BREAD PUDDING

- 1½ cups hot milk
- 3 cups cubed white or whole wheat bread
- 4 eggs, beaten
- 2 to 4 tablespoons honey
- 2½ cups milk
- ¾ cup raisins, scalded and drained
- 1 cup cottage cheese
- Ground nutmeg

Pour milk over bread in bowl and set aside to moisten. Meanwhile, combine eggs, honey, and remaining milk, stirring until blended. Arrange alternate layers of moistened bread, raisins, and cheese in greased shallow casserole, covering each layer with egg-milk mixture. Pour in remaining egg-milk mixture. Sprinkle nutmeg on top. Bake in a moderate oven (350°F.) about 45 minutes or until mixture is no longer runny when tested in the center with the tip of a knife. Makes 6 servings.

☙ HOLIDAY STEAMED PRUNE AND CRANBERRY PUDDING WITH FOAMY BRANDY SAUCE

- 1⅓ cups sifted all-purpose flour
- ½ cup sugar
- ½ teaspoon salt
- 2 teaspoons baking soda
- 1 teaspoon cinnamon
- 1⅓ cups diced pitted cooked dried prunes
- 1 cup raw cranberries
- ½ cup coarsely chopped walnuts
- ½ cup molasses
- ¼ cup warm water

Sift together flour, sugar, salt, baking soda, and cinnamon into mixing bowl. Add prunes, cranberries, and walnuts; mix thoroughly. Mix together molasses and water; add to first mixture; mix well and turn into well-greased 1-quart mold. Cover tightly. Use aluminum foil if necessary. Stand on rack in deep saucepan. Pour in boiling water around pudding to rise half-way up around mold. Cover and steam 1¼ hours. Unmold and serve hot with sauce. Makes 1 quart-size steamed pudding.

Foamy Brandy Sauce

- 2 egg yolks
- ⅛ teaspoon salt
- ¾ cup sifted confectioners' sugar
- 2 tablespoons brandy
- Few grains ground nutmeg
- ¾ cup heavy cream, whipped

Beat egg yolks with salt until light. Gradually add sugar while continuing beating until thick. Add brandy, 1 teaspoon at a time, beating well after each addition. Add nutmeg and fold in whipped cream. Serve with Steamed Pudding. Makes about 1½ cups sauce.

EASY JELLY ROLL

- ¾ cup sifted all-purpose flour
- 1 teaspoon baking powder
- ½ teaspoon salt
- 6 egg whites, at room temperature
- ¼ cup sugar
- 6 egg yolks
- ¼ cup sugar
- 1 teaspoon pure vanilla extract
- 1 tablespoon unsalted shortening
- 4 tablespoons flour
- 1½ cups jelly, mashed to spreading consistency
- Confectioners' sugar

Sift together flour, baking powder, and salt. Set aside. Beat egg whites until they are frothy; gradually add sugar, beating until stiff peaks form. Using the same unwashed beater, beat egg yolks until thick. Gradually add sugar and beat until light. Fold into beaten egg whites. Fold in sifted dry ingredients and vanilla. Combine shortening and flour and mix into a paste. Spread evenly on entire insides of 15½-x-10½-inch jelly roll pan. Pour in batter; spread evenly to the sides. Bake in moderate oven (350°F.) about 18 to 20 minutes or until golden and beginning to shrink away from sides of the pan. Remove from oven and immediately turn upside down on lightly floured paper slightly larger than the pan. Tap back of pan until cake falls out. Lift off pan. Cool cake to lukewarm; thinly slice off crispy edges all around cake. Spread with jelly evenly to within ½-inch of edges of four cake sides. Roll lengthwise without squeezing to make a snug roll. Roll in the paper and let rest on seam about 1 to 1½ hours or until set enough to slice. Sprinkle with confectioners' sugar. Cut into slices 1 to 1¼ inches thick. Makes about 10 to 12 slices.

☙ FROZEN FRESH PEACH TREAT

This is super-duper, and one of the joys of summertime if made with the fresh peaches. You should try this spooned into the center of a great big angel cake for a party.

- 1½ cups sliced fresh or frozen peaches (if using frozen peaches, omit half the sugar)
- 2 teaspoons fresh lemon or lime juice
- ⅔ cup confectioners' sugar
- 2 egg whites
- ¼ teaspoon salt
- 1½ cups heavy cream, whipped

Mash peaches to a pulp, allowing a few bits and pieces of peach to remain. Add lemon juice and sugar, stirring until blended. Beat egg whites with salt until stiff peaks form. Fold lightly into peach mixture. Gently fold in whipped cream, allowing a few patches of cream to show. Turn into ice cube tray. Freeze in freezer or refrigerator, with control set at lowest setting, until icy around the sides. Stir icy sides through mixture; place in regular refrigerator ice cube compartment, returned to normal setting, for 1½ to 2 hours, or until barely firm. Serve in sherbet glasses. Makes 6 to 8 servings.

☙ SOUTH AMERICAN LEMON DESSERT PANCAKES

You will find these South American pancakes a friend in need when you have the problem of serving a dreamy dessert to guests or even to your family. All you need are the old familiar ingredients that you have on hand all the time, and a little bit of imagination. Put them together and you have something just as glamorous as if you had shopped for fancy fixings like meringue glacé and heavy cream. I think you'll find that men go mad over these South American lemon pancakes. Don't be afraid to turn the pancakes over, because once they're brown you'll find that they are pretty manageable. If I were you I would make double the recipe because I'm sure that the diners are going to want seconds. It seems to me wherever you go, to the four corners of the earth, you'll find that people are using pancakes of some sort or another, and here in America we make them all. So now try out these from South America. This, by the way, makes enough for eight. One apiece, though.

1 cup sifted all-purpose flour
6 tablespoons sugar
⅛ teaspoon salt
1 cup water
2 eggs, beaten
3 tablespoons butter or margarine, to cook pancakes
½ cup melted butter or margarine
2 tablespoons fresh lemon juice
Confectioners' sugar
Lemon halves

Sift together flour, sugar, and salt into mixing bowl. Gradually add water while stirring to make a smooth, lumpless batter. Add eggs and beat thoroughly until blended. Heat 8-inch skillet or frying pan over moderate heat; add 1 teaspoon butter and tip the pan to spread butter evenly. Add enough batter to barely coat bottom of pan. Cook until golden brown on both sides, turning once. Lift out and keep hot. Repeat making pancakes using 1 teaspoon butter for each one. Stack the pancakes and keep hot. When pancakes are all made, stir melted butter into lemon juice. Spread over each pancake; sprinkle with confectioners' sugar and roll up tightly. Pour remaining butter-lemon mixture over finished pancakes. Serve hot with lemon halves on the side. Makes 6 to 8 servings.

◆§ BAKED SPICED APPLE SLICES

Folks just seem to go mad over recipes—dessert recipes that is—that call for apples. This one is so successful because it's very much like a pie. No need to push away the crust and just eat the filling, as so many of us do. It has practically the same spicing as apple pie filling, with a plus —the orange juice. It's a dessert of character, and looks fussy. I mean it looks as if you'd really cared about taking a little time to make dessert for dinner. I usually make a big batch and serve it warm first, and then cold with cream or a slice of cheese. It's delightful warm or cold.

4 large cooking apples
½ cup brown sugar, packed
¾ cup fine dry bread crumbs
1 teaspoon ground cinnamon
¼ teaspoon ground nutmeg
2 tablespoons soft butter or margarine
⅓ cup orange juice

Pare, core, and slice apples into eighths. Combine brown sugar, bread crumbs, cinnamon, and nutmeg. Blend. Spread 1 tablespoon butter on entire insides of 8 x 8 x 2-inch pan. Fill pan with alternate layers of apples, brown sugar mixture, and orange juice, ending with sugar mixture on top. Cover with aluminum foil. Bake in a moderate oven (375°F.) 15 minutes. Uncover and continue to bake about ½ hour longer or until apples are soft. Serve warm or cold with cream, or a la mode with ice cream. Makes 6 servings.

◆§ CHOCOLATE COVERED PEANUT CRISP

1 cup melted butter or margarine
1 cup sugar
2 tablespoons water
1 tablespoon light corn syrup
¾ cup finely chopped salted peanuts
¼ teaspoon vanilla
4 squares unsweetened chocolate, melted

Combine butter, sugar, water, and corn syrup in a medium saucepan. Stir well and place over moderate heat. Cook, stirring frequently to 290°F. on candy thermometer, or until a few drops of syrup become brittle in cold water. Remove from heat at once; add peanuts and vanilla. Mix well and pour into greased 15½ x 10½-inch pan, spreading mixture evenly over entire pan. As it hardens, pry candy loose from pan, lifting candy up all around the sides with spatula. When candy has hardened, spread one half the melted chocolate (see note) evenly over the top. Cool and chill until chocolate sets. Lift whole piece of candy over with 2 pancake turners. Melt remaining chocolate and spread over other side of candy. Cool until brittle enough to break. Break into pieces. Makes about 1¼ pounds candy.

NOTE: Melt chocolate in cup standing in hot water. Melt 2 squares for one side; melt remaining 2 squares later, as needed.

SPONGE DROPS

This recipe reminds me of a letter I received from a homemaker soon after I used it on TV. It went something like this: "Dear Josie—I made the Sponge Drops and did you say ½ cup of flour or was I mistaken? And also why did the cakes stick to the cookie sheet? When I put in the flour, the batter was on the liquid side so I added more flour—was I right or wrong?" Well, she was right in the first amount of flour. You see, she had made them before she waited to write in for the recipe. She should have used ½ cup of sifted all-purpose flour, as you can see from the recipe. She was wrong though, in that she tried to bake them on a cookie sheet, because I remember I made a point that the batter was runny and should be baked in little fluted paper cups. During baking the batter clings to the cup sides. After they are baked and allowed to stand a while, the little cakes can easily be pulled away from the paper. I wouldn't try to make them on a cookie sheet. I'd wait until I could get to the store and get some of these little fluted paper cups—the ones that you use for lining cup cake or muffin pans. Little cakes to be baked on a cookie sheet would have to be made after an entirely different recipe. In order to get a feathery light cake we had to make a batter with a minimum amount of flour. It has to depend on the sides of the pan to prevent spreading. Thus, our lady got straightened out with the recipe. She wrote again and said how glad she was that she did try them again . . . and she had so much fun because they came out right.

3 egg whites, at room temperature
¼ cup sugar
4 egg yolks
¼ cup sugar
½ teaspoon grated lemon rind
½ cup sifted all-purpose flour
2 tablespoons melted butter or margarine

Beat egg whites until frothy; gradually add ¼ cup sugar, continuing to beat until stiff peaks form. Beat egg yolks until thick; gradually add ¼ cup sugar while beating until fluffy. Add lemon rind, half of the beaten egg whites, and the flour; mix well. Add melted butter or margarine and fold in remaining beaten egg whites. Fill fluted paper bon bon cups or frilled paper cupcake liners to ⅛-inch from tops. Place cups on cookie sheet. Bake in moderate oven (350°F.) 8 to 10 minutes or until done. Makes about 3 dozen very small or 1 dozen medium Sponge Drops.

I've made a lot of cookies and I've eaten a lot of cookies, but between you and me, the Mexican Wedding Cookies are the richest and the best-tasting cookies I think I've made within the last two years. Everybody loves them and my trouble has been that I never seem to be able to make enough. The other day, months after I made this recipe, our Technical Director came back to sample some Russian Tea Cookies that had appeared on TV. After eating one he said, "Josie, these are good, but nothing like those wedding cookies you once made. I could eat myself sick over those cookies. When're you going to make them again?"

MEXICAN WEDDING COOKIES

- 1 cup soft butter or margarine
- ⅞ cup sifted confectioners' sugar
- 1⅓ cups ground walnuts
- ½ teaspoon ground cinnamon
- 1 teaspoon pure vanilla extract
- 2 cups sifted all-purpose flour
- Sifted confectioners' sugar

Stir butter until smooth and creamy; add sugar a little at a time, beating constantly. Add nuts, cinnamon, and vanilla. Gradually add flour and mix into a dough. Turn out on lightly floured surface; shape into two rolls about 2½-inches in diameter; roll each in waxed paper and refrigerate 1 hour or until firm enough to slice. To bake, slice ⅜-inch thick and place 1 inch apart on ungreased cookie sheet. Press thumb firmly through the center of each cookie to the pan, to make a ring. Bake in a moderate oven (375°F.) about 12 to 14 minutes, or until light golden and done. When cool, roll in sifted confectioners' sugar. Makes 3½ dozen.

The anise cookie is not a rich cookie, neither is it very sweet. It's perfect to go with a cup of tea and it leaves one with a great deal of satisfaction after hunting around for something that's a little tasty. I love the flavor of anise because that's the flavor that is used mostly for licorice products. As a matter of fact, the flavoring is so pungent that many cough remedies use it in the mixtures to make them palatable. Many years ago it used to be used in medicines, especially for pleurisy, and in the 9th century Charlemagne ordered anise to be grown on the Imperial farm. Anise and cumin are so old that they were mentioned in the Bible. As with many other herbs and spices, there is an old superstition about anise: it was believed that if a person slept with a sprig of fresh anise under his pillow he'd have sweet dreams. Unless you're lucky enough to have a garden and grow your own anise, you'll have to depend on the anise seed, ground or whole, as you buy it in your supermarket or store.

LUCKY ANISE SLICES

- 2 cups sifted all-purpose flour
- 1¼ teaspoons baking powder
- ¼ teaspoon salt
- ½ cup soft butter or margarine
- 6 tablespoons sugar
- 2 eggs
- ½ teaspoon ground anise seed
- ¼ teaspoon anise oil

Sift together flour, baking powder, and salt. Set aside. Stir butter until creamy and beat until light and fluffy. Add sugar gradually, beating constantly. Add eggs one at a time, beating well after each addition. Add sifted dry ingredients, anise seed, and oil, stirring until dough leaves sides of bowl. Turn onto a lightly floured surface; knead lightly and shape into 2½-inch roll. Flatten into strip ½ inch thick and 5 inches across. Place on greased cookie sheet. Bake in moderate oven (350°F.) about 20 to 25 minutes or until golden. Cool to lukewarm. Lift off pan and slice across in 1-inch slices. Place cut side down on cookie sheet. Bake in hot oven (400°F.) about 8 to 10 minutes or until toasted. Makes 12 slices.

This was a tremendously popular recipe because so many people would like to enjoy doughnuts but for some reason do not eat the fried doughnuts. These are excellent eaten hot. They should certainly not be too rich, and they are certainly not fried. Our chief prop man adored them and begged for the recipe. He prides himself on being an amateur cook and is not happy when the guests are waiting around to eat unless he's back in the kitchen seeing about the "eats" personally.

BAKED HOT BISCUIT CRULLERS

2 cups sifted all-purpose flour
3½ teaspoons baking powder
1 teaspoon salt
2 tablespoons sugar
¼ teaspoon ground cinnamon
¼ teaspoon ground nutmeg
¼ cup shortening or salad oil
⅔ cup light cream
1 egg, beaten
¼ cup melted butter or margarine
Granulated sugar

Sift together flour, baking powder, salt, sugar, cinnamon, and nutmeg into mixing bowl. Add shortening, and rub together or blend until like fine meal. Combine cream and egg; add to dry ingredients, mixing only long enough to dampen all flour. Turn out on lightly floured surface. knead into a smooth ball. Roll out about ½ inch thick; cut out with floured doughnut cutter. Place cut out "holes" on greased cookie sheet. Hold opposite sides of each doughnut with fingers of both hands, then twist to make a figure eight. Arrange on greased cookie sheet with the "holes." Bake in a hot oven (400°F.) about 10 to 12 minutes or until done. When baked, immediately dip tops in melted butter, then into granulated sugar. Makes 8 crullers and "8 holes."

CELESTIAL FAVOURS (CZECHOSLOVAKIAN)

2 cups sifted all-purpose flour
½ teaspoon salt
4 tablespoons chilled butter or margarine
2 eggs, beaten
2 tablespoons hot milk
Oil for shallow-frying
Confectioners' sugar and ground cinnamon

Sift together flour and salt into mixing bowl. Add butter; rub or cut in with pastry blender or 2 knives, until like fine meal. Add eggs and milk; stir until blended. Turn onto lightly floured surface; knead until smooth and roll into a ball. Wrap in waxed paper or foil. Refrigerate about 1 hour. Roll dough into large square, ¼ inch thick; fold two opposite sides to center, then in half like a book. Turn folded dough clockwise one quarter turn; roll again ¼ inch thick. Repeat folding and rolling 2 more times. Roll out into a ⅛-inch thick square. Cut into 3-inch squares; cut squares across from corner to corner to make triangles. Shallow-fry in hot oil (about 1½ inches deep), for about 2 minutes or until golden brown, turning once. Drain on absorbent paper. Dust with sugar and cinnamon. Serve cold. Makes approximately 1½ dozen.

SESAME SEED COOKIES

I'll never forget the uproar these cookies caused in our studio for days. This is how they began. A letter came in from one of our viewers which read something like this: "Dear Josie: I've been cooking by your recipes for quite some time now and I have a great deal of faith in you. Can you help me with this problem? There is a small Italian bakery near us and I go in there and ask for some cookies with the seeds—I'd like to make some of those cookies. But

I haven't got the nerve to ask these bakery men to divulge the recipe. Here are some of the seeds. Can you please send me the recipe." And enclosed in the letter was a little packet with about five toasted sesame seeds. That meant I had to run for my crystal ball. First of all I took myself to an Italian bakery and looked over all the cookies with sesame seed, and they had quite a few. Some were round and some were in slices and some were in bars, so I wrote this dear lady back and asked her to tell me if the cookies were round, or to give me some sort of an idea of their dimensions and what they looked like, or to describe the appearance a little bit more—which she did. It turned out that they were a round cookie covered with seeds. So then I did some testing. It seems that there's a national cookie in Italy called "Biscoti de Regina," which means Queen's biscuits. I called them Sesame Seed Cookies because I adapted the original recipe to our own American ingredients. It was a pleasure to work with sesame seed because somehow, outside of candy making and oil making, sesame had not been used much in America. It has since become well-known and used in cakes and pies. Italian bakers put it on bread; when it's toasted it has a nut-like delicious flavor. It's also used in the Jewish candy Halvah, and in the orient. As a matter of fact, it is cultivated in India and China and is a staple article of nourishment there. Sesame is classified as an herb; it grows from one to two feet high, with pretty blossoms. It's also called "Benne Seed." You can buy it unhulled and hulled, but the same nutlike flavor comes out in both hulled and unhulled after toasting. Use either one for these cookies. After you make them once or twice I believe that you're going to put them on your permanent list of cookie favorites.

- 2½ cups sifted all-purpose flour
- 1 teaspoon baking powder
- ¼ teaspoon salt
- ½ cup soft butter or margarine
- ½ cup sugar
- ¼ cup milk
- 1 egg, beaten
- 1 teaspoon pure vanilla extract
- 1 cup whole sesame seed

Sift together flour, baking powder, and salt. Set aside. Stir butter until creamy. Gradually add sugar, stirring until blended. Add milk, egg, and vanilla. Beat until blended. Gradually add sifted dry ingredients, stirring into a dough. Press into a ball and turn onto lightly floured surface. Knead until smooth. Roll in waxed paper and refrigerate about ½ hour. Place sesame seed in fine sieve. Hold under running water until thoroughly wet. Drain and spread on plate or waxed paper. Pinch off small pieces of dough and roll into walnut-sized balls. Drop into damp sesame seed, rolling them until well-coated. Flatten slightly. Place on ungreased cookie sheet 1½ inches apart. Bake in a hot oven (425°F.) 15 to 16 minutes or until done. Makes about 3½ to 4 dozen (1¼-inch) cookies.

☙ DREAM COOKIES

- 2 cups sifted all-purpose flour
- 1 teaspoon baking powder
- ½ teaspoon salt
- 1 cup butter or margarine
- ¾ cup sugar
- 2 tablespoons milk
- 2 teaspoons pure vanilla extract
- 30 to 35 blanched almonds, split into halves

Sift together flour, baking powder, and salt; set aside. Melt butter in medium saucepan and let brown slightly; remove from heat at once; stand saucepan in pan of ice water until cool. Gradually add sugar to cooled butter in saucepan, stirring constantly. Beat until fluffy; stir in milk and vanilla. Gradually add sifted dry ingredients, stirring until dough forms. Turn onto lightly floured surface. Knead lightly until smooth. Pinch off small pieces of dough and roll into walnut-sized balls. Place on lightly greased cookie sheet. Press balls slightly to flatten. Press one half almond on top of each. Bake in a very slow oven (250°F.) about 25 to 30 minutes, until golden brown and done. Makes about 5 to 6 dozen (1-inch) cookies.

BREAD CRUMB NUT BARS

- 2 eggs
- 1 cup sugar
- 1 teaspoon ground cinnamon
- ½ teaspoon salt
- ¼ cup melted butter or margarine
- 1½ cups fine dry bread crumbs
- ½ cup chopped walnuts or other nuts
- Confectioners' sugar

Beat eggs until fluffy; gradually add sugar, continuing to beat until thick and light. Stir in cinnamon, salt, and melted butter. Add bread crumbs and nuts; mix well. Turn into well-greased and floured 9 x 9 x 1¾-inch pan. Smooth and level top with back of tablespoon dipped repeatedly in cold water. Bake in a slow oven (300°F.) about 35 minutes or until done; cool and cut into 16 squares. Sprinkle with confectioners' sugar. Makes 16 nut bars.

MOIST AND SWEET BRAN MUFFINS

Without a doubt, this recipe brought in so many requests that we considered it a leader. Puzzled me because of all the glorious recipes we have for baked goodies like cakes, pies and muffins, buns, etc. I just wondered why viewers wanted me to dig up this old-fashioned raisin bran muffin. But it's a honey! I had to go on a searching trip to find bran. Supermarkets don't stock it anymore, the reason being that they have no calls for it. Women phoned and wrote: "where could they buy bran?" I bought it in a health-food store. If you live in a section where there still is a feed store, they'll have it because bran is still fed to cattle. You might check the food department in some of the glamorous super-duper department stores of today. It can generally be ordered from your grocer. There's really no technique to making these muffins; it's just a matter of measuring, stirring, and baking. It's as simple as that! They are terrific.

⧼ MOIST AND SWEET RAISIN BRAN MUFFINS

1½ cups sifted all-purpose flour
1½ teaspoons baking powder
½ teaspoon baking soda
1 teaspoon salt
1 cup bran
½ cup raisins
1 egg, beaten
¾ cup molasses
¼ cup melted shortening or oil
⅞ cup milk

Sift together flour, baking powder, baking soda, and salt into mixing bowl; stir in bran and raisins. Mix together egg, molasses, melted shortening, and milk; add all at once to dry mixture; beat 1 minute or until blended. Turn into well-greased and floured medium-size muffin pans, filling them ¾ full; bake in a hot oven (400°F.) about 22 to 25 minutes or until done. Remove from oven and let stand 1 minute. Invert on rack; tap back of pans lightly and muffins will fall out. Makes 1 dozen medium-sized muffins.

SPICE

(*Courtesy of* AMERICAN

HOW MUCH SPICE TO USE. When trying a new idea, it is safest to start with ¼ teaspoon of spice (excepting the red pepper spices) to a pint of sauce, soup or vegetables or a pound of meat, fish or fowl.

SPICE	APPETIZER	SOUP	MEAT and EGGS	FISH & POULTRY
ALLSPICE	Cocktail Meatballs	Pot Au Feu	Hamsteak	Oyster Stew
BASIL	Cheese Stuffed Celery	Manhattan Clam Chowder	Ragout of Beef	Shrimp Creole
BAY LEAF	Pickled Beets	Vegetable Soup	Lamb Stew	Simmered Chicken
CARAWAY Seed	Mild Cheese Spreads		Sauerbraten	
CINNAMON	Cranberry Juice	Fruit Soup	Pork Chops	Sweet and Sour Fish
CAYENNE	Deviled Eggs	Oyster Stew	Barbecued Beef	Poached Salmon Hollandaise
CELERY Salt and Seed	Ham Spread (Salt)	Cream of Celery (Seed)	Meat Loaf (Seed)	Chicken Croquettes (Salt)
CHERVIL	Fish Dips	Cream Soup	Omelet	Chicken Saute
CHILI Powder	Seafood Cocktail Sauce	Pepper Pot	Chili con Carne	Arroz con Pollo
CLOVES	Fruit Punch	Mulligatawney	Boiled Tongue	Baked Fish
CURRY Powder	Curried Shrimp	Cream of Mushroom	Curry of Lamb	Chicken Hash
DILL Seed	Cottage Cheese	Split Pea	Grilled Lamb Steak	Drawn Butter for Shellfish
GARLIC Salt or Powder	Clam Dip	Vegetable Soup	Roast Lamb	Bouillabaisse
GINGER	Broiled Grapefruit	Bean Soup	Dust lightly over Steak	Roast Chicken

[C]HART

[S]PICE TRADE ASSOCIATION)

ABOUT PEPPER. Our most important spice deserves special attention. So versatile is its flavor, it could play a welcome role in any dish on this chart (except desserts). Good cooks always remember pepper as a seasoning corrector, often adding a final dash to taste regardless of the other seasonings used.

SAUCES	VEGETABLES	SALAD & DRESSING	DESSERTS
Barbecue	Eggplant Creole	Cottage Cheese Dressing	Apple Tapioca Pudding
Spaghetti	Stewed Tomatoes	Russian Dressing	
Bordelaise	Boiled New Potatoes	Tomato Juice Dressing	
Beef a la Mode Sauce	Cabbage Wedges		
Butter Sauce for Squash	Sweet Potato Croquettes	Stewed Fruit Salad	Chocolate Pudding
Bearnaise	Cooked Greens	Tuna Fish Salad	
Celery Sauce (Seed)	Cauliflower (Salt)	Cole Slaw (Seed)	
[V]egetable Sauce	Peas Francaise	Caesar Salad	
Meat Gravy	Corn Mexicali	Chili French Dressing	
Sauce Madeira	Candied Sweet Potatoes		Stewed Pears
Orientale or Indienne	Creamed Vegetables	Curried Mayonnaise	
Dill Sauce for [F]ish or Chicken	Peas and Carrots	Sour Cream Dressing	
Garlic Butter	Eggs and Tomato Casserole	Tomato and Cucumber Salad	
Cocktail	Buttered Beets	Cream Dressing for Ginger Pears	Stewed Dried Fruits

SPICE CHAR

(*Courtesy of* AMERICA

SPICE	APPETIZER	SOUP	MEAT & EGGS	FISH & POULTR
MACE	Quiche Lorraine	Petite Marmite	Veal Fricassee	Fish Stew
MARJORAM	Fruit Punch Cup	Onion Soup	Roast Lamb	Salmon Loaf
MINT	Fruit Cup	Sprinkle over Split Pea	Veal Roast	Cold Fish
MUSTARD Powdered Dry	Ham Spread	Lobster Bisque	Virginia Ham	Deviled Crab
NUTMEG	Chopped Oysters	Cream DuBarry	Salisbury Steak	Southern Fried Chicken
ONION Powder, Salt, Flakes and Instant Minced Onion	Avocado Spread (Powder)	Consommes (Flakes)	Meat Loaf (Instant Minced Onion)	Fried Shrimp (Salt)
OREGANO	Sharp Cheese Spread	Beef Soup	Swiss Steak	Court Boullion
PAPRIKA	Creamed Seafood	Creamed Soup	Hungarian Goulash	Oven Fried Chicken
PARSLEY Flakes	Cheese Balls	Cream of Asparagus	Irish Lamb Stew	Broiled Mackere
ROSEMARY	Deviled Eggs	Mock Turtle	Lamb Loaf	Chicken a la Kin
SAGE	Cheese Spreads	Consomme	Cold Roast Beef	Poultry Stuffing
SAVORY	Liver Paste	Lentil Soup	Scrambled Eggs	Chicken Loaf
TARRAGON	Mushrooms a la Greque	Snap Bean Soup	Marinated Lamb or Beef	Lobster
THYME	Artichokes	Clam Chowder	Use sparingly in Fricassees	Poultry Stuffing

ONTINUED)

ICE TRADE ASSOCIATION)

SAUCES	VEGETABLES	SALAD & DRESSING	DESSERTS
Creole	Succotash	Fruit Salad	Cottage Pudding
Brown	Eggplant	Mixed Green Salad	
Lamb	Green Peas	Cottage Cheese Salad	Ambrosia
Cream Sauce for Fish	Baked Beans	Egg Salad	Gingerbread Cookies
Mushroom	Glazed Carrots	Sweet Salad Dressing	Sprinkle over Vanilla Ice Cream
Tomato (Powder)	Broiled Tomatoes (Salt)	Vinaigrette Dressing (Instant Minced Onion)	
Spaghetti	Boiled Onions	Sea Food	
aprika Cream	Baked Potato	Cole Slaw	
Chasseur	French Fried Potatoes	Tossed Green Salad	
Cheese	Sauteed Mushrooms	Meat Salad	
Duck	Brussels Sprouts	Herbed French Dressing	
Fish	Beets	Red Kidney Bean Salad	
Green	Buttered Broccoli	Chicken Salad	
Bordelaise	Lightly on Sauteed Mushrooms	Tomato Aspic	

Index

C

M

N

O

P

Fruit Salad

Dressing

1/2 cup peanut Butter
1/2 cup orange juice
1/2 cup pineapple juice
1/4 cup lemon juice
2 tablespoon Honey salt

---

for Salad.
grape fruit, apples, grape.
Bannan dip in lemon juice
so they wont turn black,
pears. pine apples, orange

Chickey, Romain
green

potatoes Cresotoll

2 lbs potatoes sliced
1 clove garlic chopped,
2 eggs, 1 cup Heavy Cream,
Salt Pepper nutmeg